Never Surrender

Never Surrender

✦

An American Navy Sailor's Struggle For Survival in the Deadly Japanese P.O.W. Camps of WW II

Earl Anderson
Shawn Davis

iUniverse, Inc.
New York Lincoln Shanghai

Never Surrender
An American Navy Sailor's Struggle For Survival in the Deadly Japanese P.O.W. Camps of WW II

iUniverse books may be ordered through booksellers or by contacting:

iUniverse
2021 Pine Lake Road, Suite 100
Lincoln, NE 68512
www.iuniverse.com
1-800-Authors (1-800-288-4677)

The views expressed in this work are solely those of the author and do not necessarily reflect the views of the publisher, and the publisher hereby disclaims any responsibility for them.

ISBN-13: 978-0-595-40739-2 (pbk)
ISBN-13: 978-0-595-85104-1 (ebk)
ISBN-10: 0-595-40739-0 (pbk)
ISBN-10: 0-595-85104-5 (ebk)

Printed in the United States of America

Earl's Dedication

For My Father,
John Ellis Anderson

Contents

Introduction xi

CHAPTER 1   U.S.S. Cincinnati 1

CHAPTER 2   U.S.S. Canopus 9

CHAPTER 3   U.S.S. Permit 17

CHAPTER 4   Ambush 23

CHAPTER 5   Mama San 29

CHAPTER 6   Battleground: Bataan 35

CHAPTER 7   Last Stand: Corregidor 49

CHAPTER 8   Surrender 63

CHAPTER 9   Camp Cabanatuan 68

CHAPTER 10   Destination: Japan 72

CHAPTER 11   Yokohama 75

CHAPTER 12   Air Raids 90

CHAPTER 13   Liberation 96

CHAPTER 14   Coming Home 101

CHAPTER 15   The Aftermath 104

Epilogue 107

Author Bios 109

Bibliography for Never Surrender 111

Acknowledgements

I {Shawn Davis} want to thank my Uncle Walter for his service to his country during WW II and for supporting and encouraging his brother, Earl, to return to the difficult memories of the past in order to enlighten future generations. I would especially like to thank Joe Masterson for his invaluable advice and guidance, which was integral to the success of this project. I would like to thank my parents, Bill and Joyce Davis, for their crucial help giving support and advice to me during the writing of this book. I want to thank my second cousins, Earl Wayne Jackson and Elise Jackson, for sending us Earl's memoir. I want to thank my best friend from high school and co-author of *American Insurrection*, Robert E. Moore, Jr. Esq. for creating the excellent cover artwork. I would like to thank my colleague, Sgt. Frank Cooney, for the superior research materials he gave me. I would also like to thank my colleague, Officer Rick Bailey, for lending me his computer expertise and providing invaluable assistance with the novel's graphics.

Introduction

In April, 2005, my father, Bill Davis, met my great uncle, Earl Anderson, at a family memorial for Earl's late wife, Penny, in Maine. Earl lived in Florida for many years, and my father lived in Massachusetts all his life, so they had only met sporadically throughout the years at rare family events. My father, a retired history teacher, knew his Uncle Earl was a WW II veteran who had been a P.O.W. of the Japanese for three and a half years. However, he had never heard any stories of Earl's POW experiences. This time, my father was able to speak with Earl extensively and became fascinated by his W.W. II adventures. My father discovered Earl had written a forty-page memoir, which he had created at the prompting of his other nephew, Earl Wayne Jackson. Earl Wayne Jackson' wife, Elise Jackson, sent Earl's memoir to my father. My dad knew I was an aspiring writer who was interested in historical drama, so he passed on the information to me. I read the memoir and was shocked and fascinated by Earl's intriguing story. As clichéd as it sounds, I decided that I had to tell his incredible story of survival to the world.

Like me, most people in my generation know very little about WW II aside from what they see in Hollywood movies such as *Saving Private Ryan*. After reading my great uncle's story, I was shocked by the extent of the brutality used by Japanese soldiers against captured American POWs I was also inspired by the heroism and ingenuity that the American POWs used to survive in the deadly Japanese internment camps. Sadly, this was mostly new information for me. Since I was a kid, I always knew from watching movies that the German Nazis of WW II were some villainous, ruthless bastards. I guessed that, like me, most Americans already knew about Nazi atrocities such as the brutal German extermination camps of WW II from watching movies like *Schindler's List* and television documentaries on PBS. But, I also guessed that most Americans, like me, did not know about Japanese atrocities like the Nanking Massacre, where over 300,000 Chinese men, women, and children were systematically tortured and annihilated. After speaking with many friends and acquaintances, I found out I was right. Before reading my great uncle's memoir, I never knew that the average Japanese soldier during WW II often made the average German soldier look like a Boy

Scout by comparison. I was shocked to discover that in many instances, the psychopathic Japanese soldiers "out-Nazied" the Nazis!

To add insult to injury, the Japanese government has never apologized for its WW II atrocities against the Chinese, Korean, Filipino, American, and British people. In fact, some Japanese scholars changed the history books in Japan so the Nanking Massacre of 300,000 Chinese civilians in just a few weeks was downplayed and renamed the "Nanking Incident." Some Japanese scholars deny the massacre ever happened despite the testimony of thousands of Chinese civilians and foreigners who were trapped in the city. Recently, the Japanese Prime Minister visited a shrine for Japan's supposed "war heroes." To put this action in perspective, it would be like the German Prime Minister visiting a shrine in Berlin dedicated to Hitler and his henchmen.

This was just one of the many shocking revelations included in my great uncle's incredible story. I decided that it was my duty, as an aspiring writer, to bring his story to light in order to destroy people's ignorance, like my own, of Japanese atrocities and American heroism in the face of such atrocities. So, in May, 2005 I flew down to Florida to visit my great uncle.

Meeting my Great Uncle Earl in person was one of the most poignant experiences of my life. To actually come face-to-face with the intrepid man who had endured hardships beyond what most people could even imagine was inspiring. My father, Bill Davis, came with me on my journey. My great uncle Earl and his younger {82 yrs old} brother, Walter, met us at the airport and drove us back to Earl's house in Summerfield, Florida. Earl and Walter joked together like an improvised comedy team during most of the ride. They had my dad and I laughing at the way they kidded each other and in colloquial terminology, "busted each other's balls" for the sheer fun of it. It reminded me of something my friends and I would do.

The four of us went out to dinner that night at a local restaurant. My great uncle was 86 years old, but he smiled easily and had a boyish quality that was very endearing. He was in great shape and looked as fit as any fifty year old. The first thing Earl did when we arrived was to start kidding around with the waiter. It was clear that he had an appreciation for all the little joys in life that most of us took for granted. He and Walter continued to kid each other during dinner, but soon, the conversation turned serious. Earl and Walter began talking about Earl's POW experiences. At that time, the joking stopped and they became different people. My Uncle Walter seemed to know almost as much as Earl about his experiences, which led me to believe he had been a very strong supporter and confidante to Earl. It turns out I was right. There is no doubt that Walter's encouragement and support helped Earl to find the inner strength after all these years to return to his traumatic memories as a POW.

During our stay, my dad and I compiled close to twenty hours of interviews with my great uncle, recording them on a state-of-the-art micro-recorder. Most of the interviews took place in his den, but some occurred in noisy restaurants, which were obviously more difficult to interpret as I sat down to write the book. There were times during the writing of the book that I listened to my great uncle's deep, gravelly voice saying the same thing twenty or thirty times until I knew I had it right. I wanted to keep the story in Earl's own voice as much as possible, so I tried to use direct quotes as much as I could. I asked Earl many questions, so he could elaborate on various parts of his forty-page memoir. The personal interviews with my great uncle greatly enhanced my understanding of Earl's experiences and made them more real to me.

Writing my great uncle's story was challenging because he did not tell his story in chronological order. Earl told my father and I many poignant anecdotes about his WW II experiences, which I eventually had to piece together as best as I could as if I was doing a complex puzzle. My job was basically to put the anecdotes in chronological order, make the separate anecdotes flow smoothly together, add historical detail through research, add additional descriptions of exotic places in the story like Bataan and Corregidor, and make them all flow seamlessly together as if my great uncle had written the entire book from start to finish. It was a daunting, but deeply rewarding job.

The incredible story of survival you are about to read *Never Surrender* is my Great Uncle Earl Anderson's story. I tried to use Earl's direct language as much as possible in the story in order to maintain its integrity. However, since I had to physically put pen to paper for the majority of the book, much of the style, storytelling methods, and descriptions are my own. The description of the attacks at Pearl Harbor, Cavite Naval Yard, Guadalcanal, Iwo Jima, and Okinawa were obtained from my research. I obtained the quotes from Captain Sackett and Hank Henderson through research and I wove them appropriately into my great uncle's story in order to add important relevant information. I had to slightly modify sections of my great uncle's forty-page memoir to make them flow smoothly with the various anecdotes I recorded. My dad and I also called my great uncle several times to ask him questions, so I could put more detail into various sections of the book. I also sent him typed questions, which he answered and I inserted into the book in the appropriate sections.

All in all, it was an incredibly rewarding project that changed my life. It gave me a new appreciation for the many freedoms our country offers that I used to take for granted every day. It made me realize that heroes like my Great Uncle Earl are the only reason I am living in a free country. I now know that if it were not for the sacrifices my great uncle and his generation made for us, we would all be speaking German and Japanese in a brutal totalitarian state. Earl's story inspired me to learn more about WW II and to truly appreciate the sacrifice those heroic Americans made for us so we can all be free.

1

U.S.S. Cincinnati

May 28th, 1942. I'm trying to sleep. I'm lying on the ground in the pouring rain. If I roll over onto my back, the rain pummels my face. If I roll over onto my stomach, I have a face full of mud. I haven't eaten anything in days. The hunger pains are unbearable. I never thought I could survive this long without eating. Last night, I was one of seventy-five men packed into a train so tight we had to stand shoulder-to-shoulder. The train stopped and they brought us to an abandoned schoolyard. I guess the Japs thought it was a good holding pen for us because there was a high fence around it.

Suddenly, I hear shouting in Japanese. I figure it must be time for us to get up and begin our twenty-mile hike to the prison camp. Despite my weakened condition, I stand shakily to my feet. We are all in such weakened states from malnutrition; some of the guys are having trouble standing up. A Japanese officer spots two American POWs who are unable to stand. He draws a samurai sword from a scabbard on his belt and slices off their heads with two vicious strokes. Blood spurts from the stumps of their necks like fountains as their heads drop into the mud. Their swaying bodies collapse, soaking the ground with blood. I now know I will be lucky to make it to my twenty-third birthday.

I don't know how I am able to survive the hellish twenty-mile hike to the camp. I am so tired, hungry, and dehydrated that I feel like I'm walking on air when we near the end. I barely make it to the camp without collapsing. The thought of what happened to the two POWs at the schoolyard helps keep me going.

When we arrive at the entrance to the camp, we see four American POWs tied to stakes. Apparently, they were placed there as an example for trying to escape. They are in horrible conditions. They must have been there for days. Their gaunt bodies look like skeletons with skin stretched tightly over them. I feel like throwing up, but there is nothing in my stomach.

How did I get into this situation? How did I go from a happy-go-lucky young Navy sailor to a starving POW? I could say it all started on December 7th when Pearl Harbor was attacked. At the time, I was working on a submarine base in the Philippines. As the Japanese advanced, the Marines destroyed the base and we escaped on school buses. We drove to Manila and I was brought aboard the *U.S.S. Canopus*, a submarine tender. The *Canopus* was the last American ship left in Manila harbor. The rest of the fleet had fled south. If we had tried to escape then, would we have made it? Supposedly, we were too slow to get away. When the Japanese over-ran the Philippines, we were captured after a long, brutal fight on the island of Corregidor, where we made our last stand. I guess if I go way back, the event that started the chain reaction bringing me to my current predicament started in 1938.

Nineteen thirty-eight was a big year in my life: I enlisted in the U.S. Navy January 26th with high hopes of making it a career. Most importantly, I wanted to get out of the house, be on my own, and obtain some independence. I came from a large family—the Anderson family, the parents of which were immigrants from Sweden. My name is Earl Gustav Anderson. Most people call me "Andy," short for Anderson. I had twelve siblings; eight brothers and four sisters. The house was crowded.

The first day at Newport training boot camp, I wanted out. We slept in hammocks that were strung six feet above the deck. Getting into the bunks was not the hard part. It was the "getting out" that soured me on the Navy.

On the first morning, we had Reveille. If you were not out when the bugle sounded, a big Pollack lifted you out of your hammock with a baseball bat. He was the huge Chief Master-at-Arms and he ruled the barracks with an iron hand. The temperature outside was in the 20's. In the toilet and bath area, all windows were open. There were no toilet seats, so you wasted no time doing your thing. Ten minutes later, you were outside for muster, marched to the mess hall for breakfast, and then marched twenty minutes back to the barracks. At 6am, you lined up for your physical, haircut, clothes-issue, and then shots. My God! What were they all for!

The second day was the dentist thing. We lined up and four dentists worked on us in an open room. Each dentist had two Corpsmen in attendance. The guy just ahead of me was from Brooklyn, New York. He was tough-as-nails. But, when he was called, he fainted and hit the floor. The two Corpsmen had to pick him up and carry him to the dentist's chair. All his upper teeth were knocked out in the fall. The dentist pulled all the stubs out. I was next, but I knew I would be okay because I already had my teeth fixed by my family dentist, McDonald, DDS.

When I sat in the dentist chair, I informed him, "I'm all set, because I already had all my teeth fixed." The x-ray showed that I had fourteen teeth filled out of twenty-seven. With no Novocain, he proceeded to drill out all fourteen fillings, because he said they had been done wrong. I was in the chair for an hour. I swore that I would never complain about dental problems after that. For eight and a half years, I never did.

The first liberty was after four weeks. The uniform for the day was long underwear {wool-very itchy}, undress blues, high-top shoes, leggings, sweater, pea-coat, and rainwear. My uniform weighed almost as much as I did. The walk to the YMCA was about three miles. Nobody would have anything to do with us. Apparently, this area was a bad place for sailors. Strangely, we met a gal that was willing, but where do you go with all the clothes we were wearing?

I got through boot camp and had a two-week stay in the hospital for dengue fever. I missed my brother Roy's wedding. I was going to be his best man. I was in the top 10% of the class, so I was assigned to school. I chose machinist school in Norfolk, VA. It turns out it was another mistake, after my initial mistake of joining the Navy in the first place.

Before school started, four of us took the Naval Academy prep school test. We all passed, but I was ineligible because I'd be three months over 21 years old at the start of the Naval Academy. My Congressman {Bates} never answered my request to waiver the three months, so that was another strike for me. I spent five months learning the machinist trade. During that time, I made one liberty in Norfolk. The local people hated anyone in uniform. They made signs in Norfolk, reading "SAILORS AND DOGS-KEEP OFF THE GRASS". I spent weekends when I could in Washington DC, which was a great liberty town for sailors. The gals paid for everything. I guess there was a man shortage there.

Next, was the cruiser, *U.S.S. Cincinnati* in Brooklyn, NY. When I reported aboard, the Chief said, "Oh, you're a school boy."

I found out what he meant when I was permanently assigned to be a mess cook {K.P.}. Apparently, he didn't much care for "school boys." Four months later, after Atlantic maneuvers with the West Coast fleet that came via the Panama Canal, I was still mess cooking. I had to serve twenty men, family-style.

A typical day mess cooking started at 5am, serving at 5:30am, coffee, clean-up, set-up. Set-up consisted of drawing plates, bowls, cups, knives, forks, and spoons out of the scullery. I had to carry these supplies down two separate ladders for a total of 300 feet. I also had to set up the tables, which were stored overhead.

Then, I served galley food until everyone was satisfied. There were many trips back and forth. I think I lost about 20 pounds.

I asked the mess captain when I was going to be relieved of K.P. duty. His answer was "when your enlistment is up."

That did it for me. I served the mess captain one serving, but I refused to go back for seconds for him. I informed him the reason was because the cooks, who dished out the food, told me there were only enough servings for twenty men {the exact number I was serving}. When I was serving coffee, I was filling his cup and I *accidentally* forgot to stop pouring. The cup overflowed and hot coffee spilled into his lap. He jumped up from his seat and his face was flushed red with anger. I was waiting for him. I knew I would never throw the first punch because he was an officer. I pretended to act contrite and apologized to him.

He said, "You're not sorry, Anderson, you son-of-a-bitch."

He swung at me first. I ducked from the punch, swung at him, and nailed him right on the beak. A few more punches were thrown and the guys broke it up.

My Chief growled at me, "I'm going to put you on report."

"Well, if you think you can make it stick, go ahead." I responded, defiantly.

Although he threw the first punch, he put me on report. Since we were at sea, a Mutiny charge was added to the list. I went to mast and Captain Logan read the charges to me. Logan was a little guy. Most of the Captains and Admirals were little guys. Why, I don't know.

Captain Logan took one look at me and said, "Summary Court Martial. All fourteen specifications."

At that point, I didn't give a damn. I figured they could throw me out of the Navy or do whatever they want. At that time, I hated the Navy anyway.

My friends told me I had to put up a defense. The best sea lawyer on the ship was Lieutenant Carter. I went down to see him and he took my case. I went to the Court Martial and everything was "cut and dry'. The officers who served on the court also served under the Captain of the ship, so they weren't going to do anything but convict me. There were three officers there and an ensign, who was recording the trial. The witnesses against me came in and read their statements.

I said to my counselor, "They're lying! They're lying!" and I tried to get up, but he pulled me down.

He said, "Sit down. Don't say nothing."

Then, my witnesses came in and read their statements.

When it was all over, I said, "I guess I'm dead."

He said, "No, don't worry about it."

I was convicted and sentenced to six months in jail and a Bad Conduct Discharge.

The next day my notice from Washington came in and I had to go to mast to be "read off". My Chief had to go with me. I thought I was going to be thrown in jail. My skipper, Captain Logan, was nicknamed "Court Martial Logan". I remember he had a lot of hair growing out of his nose.

He looked at me angrily and said, "All charges are dismissed. Anderson, don't ever come up in front of me again. You're dismissed."

I saluted, turned around, and walked away with a big smile on my face.

Luckily, all Court Martials had to be reviewed in Washington. They threw the case out, just like my lawyer said they would. There were too many discrepancies in the testimony.

One time, we pulled into Guantanamo Bay, Cuba with five other cruisers. For the first couple of days we were anchored, they allowed us to go swimming. After that, the water got too polluted to swim in because of the discharge from the ships. There was a swimming call, so I put my swimming trunks on and went up to the top deck.

I asked my Chief, "What are those guys doing with the guns?"

He said, "Well, they are there to chase the sharks away."

When the sharks came too close to the swimmers, the lookouts would shoot the sharks. I never went swimming off a ship again.

In 1939, the fleet exercises were over and we went on a recreation cruise terminating in Tampa, FL. I was still a mess cook and still serving first servings at Gitmo {Guantanamo Bay}. Admiral Stark was due to inspect the eight cruisers he commanded. Admiral Stark was in charge of Cruiser Division Three, but he eventually became the Chief of Naval Operations in August, 1939. He presided over the expansion of the Navy from 1940-41. Ours was the first inspection of the next day. I dreamed up a plan. First, I paid the scullery man $5.00 to give me all new crockery and silverware. Second, I holystoned and polished my tables and benches, which cost me $2.00, with help. Third, I bought a new jumper, pants, undershirt, hat, and shoes for $10.00. Fourth, I swapped with a fellow cook that has his mess at the foot of the ladder leading to our area. I spent $20.00 total {a month's pay}.

I knew higher-ranked officers had good relations with enlisted men. I figured that if Admiral Stark came down to our area, I would be the first person he would see. And lo and behold, that is what happened.

He said to me, "How do you like mess cooking, son?"

That was all he had to say because my answer was short and sweet. "I don't, sir."

He asked, "Why?"

I replied, "I thought it was an unwritten rule in the Navy that three months was all that a man should serve as a mess cook."

He agreed with me and turned to our Skipper and said, "Take care of this."

He smiled at me and moved on. Down the line of command, heads nodded.

When it came to my Chief, he said, "You S.O.B.". I never served another meal and I couldn't have felt happier.

We were two days out from Tampa when they put a draft notice on the bulletin board for the Asiatic Station. They listed all kinds of ratings that they needed and I didn't qualify. Like me, my friend, Jimmy Garner, was also in trouble all the time. We decided to put our names in anyway to try to get transferred off the ship. We applied by filling out the proper forms so they could put them on file.

While we were filling out the paperwork, our Chief came down and said, "What the hell are you two guys doing?"

We said, "Well, we're putting in for the Asiatic draft, so we can get the hell off this ship."

The Chief said, "Go back to work. I'll make sure you guys get transferred to the Asiatic Station."

The *Henderson* and the *U.S.S. Chaumont* left Norfolk, Virginia and arrived in Tampa, Florida during April of 1939. There hadn't been a Navy ship in Tampa since World War I. It was an open city for us sailors and they were having all kinds of celebrations. The city treated us like sons; everything was free. A sailor could not spend a nickel. This lasted for five days.

I was off to Norfolk, VA, where I reported aboard the *U.S.S. Henderson* {a Naval transport}. The *Henderson* and the *U.S.S. Chaumont* were traveling from Norfolk, VA to the China station. The round trip would be about six months. The *Henderson* carried a crew of 300. Passengers were used to stand watches. We had 500 Marines, 800 sailors, and 400 dependants: 2000 in all.

The day after reporting in at Norfolk, VA, myself and a friend of mine, Jimmy Garner, chose to take leave and meet the ship in San Francisco. It was a thirty-day leave and ten-day travel. Wow! We had $2.65 between us, although I had $150 in the bank at home, and off we went. We began hitchhiking to Everett, Massachusetts. Today, I'd be afraid to go into a McDonalds with that amount of money. On our first try, two gals picked us up and after staying with them for two days, with them paying for everything, we had to leave heading North. The rest of the trip was uneventful. We arrived in Everett, MA on April 25, 1939, Now, how's that for memory.

May 1st, 1939. We said goodbye to all and mama said, after hugging and kissing me, "Earl, the only advice I can give you is, 'Let your conscience be your guide.'"

I knew what she meant. As far as I know, I've lived up to it to this day. That was the last time I saw my mama.

We hitchhiked out to New York and spent two days at the World's Fair. I saw my first television there. Then, we hitchhiked down to Baltimore, Maryland. We stayed in a fleabag motel in Baltimore, which cost us fifty cents for the night. Back then, we didn't have all the interstate highways we have today. The main highway going east and west was route 40. Route 40 went west all the way across the country from Baltimore to California.

On our cross-country trip to Kansas, a couple gave us a ride from Baltimore to within 20 miles of our destination. They paid for the motel, food, and everything. I started to feel good about people again. We hitchhiked to Wichita, Kansas and stayed at Jimmy Garner's aunt and uncles', who owned a dry cleaning business on North Waco Drive. They let us use one of their panel trucks for transportation. They even supplied a mattress for the back. How nice!

May 3rd, 1939. Next door to where we stayed, there were four friendly women ranging in age from 14-22 years old. This proved to be our lucky days. We didn't have to go looking. That's the first time I found out what good sex was all about. Kansas at that time was dry, but there were many speakeasies and plenty of moonshine. I drank very little, but I tried everything, which was, after all, part of my training.

Our leave was soon up. Only 18 days. How sad. People in Kansas had a different way of living, unlike New England. I enjoyed myself more in Kansas than in any other place up to that time. This was what I liked most about the Navy; interesting leaves and the temporary freedom from military discipline.

May 18th, 1939. We left Wichita and got a ride to Colorado with a truck driver. A strange guy gave us a ride to central Colorado and dropped us off in the middle of nowhere at 11:00pm. We were actually glad, because he had acted so strange! He was talking a lot of ragtime {weird, aggressive talk}. It was cold, so we built a fire in the middle of the road to keep warm and be highly visible to approaching cars. At about 3:00am, we located an abandoned car, where we spent the rest of the night.

The next day, we arrived in Denver, went to the recruiting station, and borrowed $5.00 from the Chief, a nice guy. We sent it back to him later. We hitchhiked to Salt Lake City, Utah, but we got stuck there. No drivers would pick us up. It was now Friday and our leave was up at 8:00am Monday morning at Fort Mason Dock in San Francisco.

A hobo came along and told us to follow him, as there was an express freight train leaving in one hour for Oakland, California. We hopped the freight train and stayed with about 40 hobos, most of whom were miners who worked the hard rock mines, went to Chicago, blew their wad, and were now going back to work. They got off en route to California. We spent Friday and Saturday night in a boxcar. Everyone took their shoes off with the door closed. We had a stinky good time. They shared food, coffee, and whatever advice they had. They were a great bunch of guys. I never forgot that trip.

In Oakland, CA, we had to get off the train, as it was slowing down. It was quite a feat, but the hobos showed us how. The railroad cops were making arrests. We escaped and went to the nearest gas station, changed clothes, and took a Marine bath; splashing ourselves with water. It was early Sunday morning. We hitched a ride over the new Oakland Bay Bridge, which had just opened. The man who gave us a ride was Japanese. Here we were in San Francisco, but broke, Sunday morning and hungry. We walked up Market St. and at the cross in the road, there was a candy and cigar stand that was open. We asked the guy if there was a nearby hockshop. He said, "I'll take whatever you have to hock." All we had were two pea coats and two watches, which we gave him for $15.00. Wow, we were rich. He showed us where to eat, telling us "across the street, down two stores." We took his advice, went in, and had all we could eat for seventeen cents each. It was the best meal I had in days.

The second World's Fair of 1939 was at Treasure Island, formally Goat Island, which was owned by the U.S. Navy. We reserved a room at the YMCA for twenty-five cents a night, which included a clean bed, shower, towels, and soap. What a bargain! That day we took in the World's Fair and then went back to the YMCA for a good night's rest. It felt good to sleep in a real bed for a change.

2

U.S.S. Canopus

The next day was Monday. Our ship was not at Fort Mason Dock, but was at Mare Island 40 miles away. We hitched to Vallejo and arrived late at 9:00am, just 2 hours over leave. The ship was just pulling out, headed for Fort Mason Dock in San Francisco. So, we retraced our steps and went back to Frisco. We made it to Frisco in time and reported aboard at noon. The ship left San Francisco that afternoon about 4:00pm. What a ship! There were no sleeping arrangements! We had to sleep on the deck anywhere we could find space. I never realized it would be nearly six years before I would see the Golden Gate Bridge again!

There were two or three hundred Marines on deck, who had just got out of boot camp. They were all seasick. The Pacific Ocean was as smooth as glass, and here they were leaning over the side throwing up. The Atlantic Ocean could get rough, but the Pacific was usually peaceful.

As luck would have it, I met Eddie Smith, friend of the family, who was in charge of the washrooms. He had 11 years in the Navy. All hands were allowed one bucket of fresh water for showering per day. Eddie ran all the crap and card games in the washroom and I was allowed to use the shower whenever I needed. He and the Chief Master of Arms cut the pots for the ship's welfare fund, quite a deal. The welfare fund was for enlisted men,"hardship cases", I never had to use it.

It took seven days to get to Honolulu. I went ashore and got drunk on Ocule-how, a native drink. Somehow, I cut my foot at Waikiki beach. I never expected to get an injury at such a beautiful beach. The next stop was Guam after 18 days of sailing. Then, we were on to Manila, capitol of the Philippines. Eight days later, we arrived. We stayed at Manila for two days and then went on to Shanghai, China.

The main job of the Asiatic fleet was to defend the Philippines and Guam, but we were also charged with enforcing the "Open Door Policy" in China. The Open Door Policy was maintaining equal commercial and industrial rights for people of all countries in China. Specifically, we were protecting U.S. business interests in China.

We sailed from Shanghai to Chinwontao in northern China. The Great Wall comes all the way down to the sea there. All Navy supplies came here and were trans-shipped by rail to Peking, China. Most of China's coast was under Japanese control. Chinwontao was not. We stopped at Chefoo, which was a U.S. destroyer base. Then, we stopped at Tsingtao, a submarine base, both were just places to anchor. This is where I got off and transferred to the *U.S.S. Canopus*.

The Captain of the *U.S.S. Canopus* was Commander Bannerman. Commander Earl Sackett eventually replaced him. Captain Sackett wrote a detailed account of the adventures of the *Canopus* and her crew during her final mission in the Philippines. He described the *Canopus* in his narrative;

> Built in 1921 to be a combination freight and passenger carrier for the Grace Line, she was shortly taken over by the Navy, and converted to a submarine tender. She was given extensive machine shops, foundries, and storerooms to provide for the material needs of the "pig boats", cabins and living spaces for comfort of their crews when off duty, and a few guns as a concession to the fact that she was now a man-of-war.
>
> In 1925, the *Canopus* escorted a division of six "S" type submarines of the vintage of World War I to the China Station. This imposing force, before the clouds of World War II gathered on the horizon, carried a large share of the burden of showing the Stars and Stripes in Asiatic ports, much of the time in the midst of "incidents" brought on by the spread of the New Order. {Captain E.L. Sackett, U.S.N., "The Canopus", p.1}

The six "S" type submarines accompanying the *Canopus* were the *S-36, S-37, S-38, S-39, S-40, and S-41*. The "New Order" was the Japanese attempt to reorganize all the countries of Asia so they would be subservient to Japan.

July 9th, 1939. We were getting checked in and my Chief looked at my record. He said, "Who the hell are you? I don't need you."

I was a Fireman 3rd class, which meant I couldn't stand any watches by myself.

So, he said, "Tomorrow you're a Fireman 2nd class." I was promoted on the spot.

The second day, I was given an exam for promotion, which I easily passed, but I still had no practical experience. The next day I was on the watch list 04:00-08:00 in the fire room, mind you, I had never been in a fire room which contains all the boilers that generate steam. I was awakened at 03:45 and I went to the fire room, thinking I would be with another man to show me what to do.

The man I relieved said to me when I arrived, "Are you my relief?"

I said yes and he left me in this strange place by myself.

There were four boilers that had steam up to 300lb/sq in. Only one burner was on, which at that time of day was enough to service the whole ship. Everything on the *Canopus* was run by steam. There were no electric motors to speak of. I knew what I had to do, which was to keep the water in the boilers and maintain the steam pressure. Simple, right? Yes, if you know how. Everything was okay until 05:00, when the baker called on the phone, told me he needed oil for his ovens, and hung up. I looked and found only one pump that was labeled "service". I started it up right away. The baker called and said he had enough oil. I shut the pump down, not the switch mind you, but two valves. I looked up at the boiler that was online. I saw the steam pressure and water level dropping steadily. Those boilers were 25 feet high, 12 feet wide, and 10 feet wide. There were four.

I found the water supply valve {the check valve} and opened it a little. Water level came up, but not too much. I cinched down on it and it stabilized. Now, steam pressure was dropping. This meant I had to cut in another burner on the online boiler. There were no instructions, but I managed to light the second burner. I knew nothing about flareback, but I soon found out. A sheet of flame shot right by me for about five feet; scary. From 05:00 to 07:45 when I was relieved, I had four boilers online, which consisted of 12 burners. Wow! I must have lost 20 pounds on that watch, as the temperature there was 140 degrees. In order to survive, I had to stand directly under a blower most of the time.

When the Chief found out about what happened, he said "I have Petty Officers 1st class who can't do what you did."

So, I was his fair-haired boy from then on. I was now a Fireman 2nd class E-3 and made $54 per month. What am I going to do with all this money? We were paid every two weeks in U.S. currency. When we went on liberty, we exchanged it for Chinese money at an 8 to 1 ratio. Fifteen cents of this money could buy you a full course dinner, so you can see I was living high.

At that time, in 1939, we were operating out of Tsingtao, China. Japan had occupied Tsingtao since World War 1. Prior to that, it was under German control. All businesses were German. The three cabarets were all staffed by Russians, who left Russia after the revolution. Some pretty ballerinas worked us sailors. I drank a lot of Tsingtao Beer, which is still the best beer made in China today. I had my own rickshaw coolie, who I treated the way I would have liked to be treated. I paid him $1.00 a day, bought his meals, and on one occasion visited him and his family. They thought I was the second coming. Wow! How poor they were!

By 1939, the Japanese had already taken over half of Shanghai and some of the International Settlement in China. They had already gone up to Nanking, China and wiped that city out. Most of China was under their control. The Asian countries had been fighting a losing war against the invading Japanese armies since 1931. By comparison, the U.S. didn't enter the war until ten years later in 1941.

The Japanese made their first move by attacking Manchuria in 1931. In 1933, they officially withdrew from the League of Nations. In 1937, they attacked China. Needless to say, this unprovoked aggression strained Japan's relations with China's allies, most notably, the U.S. The atrocities committed by the Japanese Army in Nanking in 1937 were never widely publicized until years later.

The Japanese Army initiated the Nanking Massacre as a retributive action against the Chinese for putting up such a strong resistance in the Battle of Shanghai. It is estimated that the Chinese killed about 40,000 of the invading Japanese during the Battle of Shanghai, while the Chinese army lost more than 200,000. The Japanese had planned on taking Shanghai in three days and all of China in three months. Instead, it took almost three months {August 13th, 1937-November 12th, 1937} to take Shanghai. The Battle of Shanghai involved bloody hand-to-hand combat in an urban setting, where both sides suffered severe attrition. The Japanese were infuriated by the massive losses inflicted by the Chinese, who they regarded as an inferior race. The Chinese wanted to show the western powers that they could mount a significant defense against the invading Japanese. They hoped their heroic actions in the Battle of Shanghai would inspire the U.S. and Britain to enter the war on China's side. Of course, that never happened. Instead, the Japanese retaliated for their massive losses by annihilating the city of Nanking.

The Japanese Army engaged in a number of atrocities in the Nanking Massacre, including mass murder, rape, theft, and arson. Immediately following the invasion of Nanking on December 13th, 1937, Japanese soldiers captured thousands of Chinese men {mostly civilians}, who were systematically executed by machine-gunning them into mass graves. For the next six weeks, mass killings of civilians {including women and children} and POWS continued. An order was sent down from the Japanese high command to execute all POWs. Civilians who tried to escape from the city were also machine-gunned. Many of the Chinese people were machine-gunned and their bodies were thrown into the Yangtze River to be carried down to Shanghai. Crowds of civilians trying to escape down the river on rafts were shot and blown up with grenades. Large crowds of civilians {including women and children} were doused with gasoline and shot, causing their bodies to ignite and catch fire. Witnesses also recalled Chinese people who were burned to death, nailed to trees, hung by their tongues from trees, and women who had their breasts cut off. Hand grenades were thrown into civilian crowds. Sometimes, the Japanese soldiers would drive crowds of civilians into the river and blow them up with grenades. Other groups of civilians and POWs were buried alive.

Some of the atrocities were considered sport by many of the Japanese soldiers. Chinese civilians and POWs were used as live bayonet practice. Contests were held to see which soldiers could decapitate more people. Some of these contests appeared in Japanese newspapers. There were reports of Japanese soldiers becoming exhausted from decapitating people. Eyewitnesses also reported instances of Japanese soldiers throwing Chinese babies into the air and catching them on their bayonets. Witnesses recalled that Japanese soldiers often bayoneted pregnant women in the stomach. The worst recorded incident was a Japanese soldier who ripped the fetus from a pregnant woman and carried it around on the tip of his bayonet. His commanding officer laughed when he saw what he had done. Japanese soldiers were reported to be laughing while they carried out these atrocities. Their commanding officers thought it was a way for them to let off steam and also to reduce the population that had to be fed when they took over. Photographic evidence confirms many of these gruesome facts. Some pictures show murdered Chinese infants and toddlers strewn across the ground in bloody piles.

It is estimated that somewhere from 20,000 to 80,000 women were raped during the Nanking Massacre. The Japanese soldiers systematized rape, so they would go door-to-door, searching for young women. Witnesses said it was common for women to be killed by mutilation after being raped. It was also reported that women were raped during the day in front of their families. Many women were forced to become "comfort women" or prostitutes for the Japanese military. The Japanese government directly sanctioned this system of organized military prostitution. Some witnesses described instances where families were forced to perform incest for the amusement of the Japanese soldiers. Other witnesses said Chinese men were forced to rape corpses.

Following the fall of the city, Japanese soldiers were given a free hand at looting. They set government buildings and civilian homes on fire. It is estimated that as much as two thirds of the city was destroyed. The Nanking War Crimes Tribunal estimated the death toll to be from 200,000 to 300,000 people killed. The extent of the massacre and the death toll from the massacre is still debated today. The Japanese government has refused to apologize for the Nanking Massacre and other World War II atrocities. Some Japanese writers deny the massacre ever happened. Japanese textbooks were rewritten to describe the massacre as a minor incident. Many Japanese textbooks refer to it as the "Nanking Incident". The Chinese built a Memorial Hall for the many victims of the massacre in Jiangdongmen, which was one of the sites where thousands of human bones were excavated. The Chinese call these mass graves "wan ren keng", or "pit of ten thousand corpses". Wan ren keng were found in many Japanese occupied areas of China after the war.

In 1988, I made a trip to Red China. We hired a tour guide to take us into Nanking. I asked him, "How many people were killed?" He simply stated, "They killed everybody." According to the tour guide, "everybody" consisted of 400,000 men, women, and children slaughtered by the invading Japanese army. Official records estimate between 200,000-300,000 people were killed in the Nanking massacre. The exact number will never be known.

After the attack on Nanking in 1937, the Japanese sunk an American Navy gun-boat, the *U.S.S. Panay*. Apparently, the gunboat had a lot of newspapermen on it that had witnessed the atrocities committed by the Japanese army in Nanking. The Japanese could not allow these men to tell the story to the world, so they sunk the boat. The United States responded by placing diplomatic and economic sanctions on Japan.

During the daytime in Tsingtao, China, I did a lot of horseback riding and even bought a pony. I kept the pony at Ma Brown's and her husband, who were Russians. The Germans had forts up to World War 1 to defend Shantung {silk} province, which the Browns now owned and this was where their stables were located. There was some beautiful scenery in this area. All the forts had been deactivated. Nighttime activity was making the rounds of the cabarets, all three; Charleston, Kismet, and the Moulin Rouge. Liberty was up at 24:00, but there were ways to extend it to overnight. Of course, the name of the game was sex. Russian refugees staffed these cabarets. Most were very attractive, especially after midnight.

Riots broke out between American sailors and Japanese troops. Many people were injured—the Asiatic fleet went on full-time alert. The Japanese sent three cruisers {old}, which they captured from Russia in 1906 during the Russo-Japanese war. The Houston {American heavy cruiser} came into port with all turrets manned and aimed at the Japanese cruisers.

The Japanese admiral's barge went alongside of the Houston—big conference—then it all quieted down. We were restricted {the whole Asiatic fleet} for a week. It seems like it all happened over some women. Some sailors played grab-ass with a Jap officer's gal, and a fight broke out. We thought that war was going to break out at that time.

The incident that started all the excitement happened in a section of Tsingtao called the "Strand Beach", which was a sailor's hangout. A couple of Japanese officers brought their girlfriends into a bar frequented by American sailors. Some sailor grabbed one of their girlfriends by the ass, which started an argument. A large riot ensued.

I was at the Navy Club at the time. An American Lieutenant was handing out bottles and calling taxicabs for soldiers to go up to the Strand Beach to participate in the riot. I never did take up the offer.

The following week, some crazy Marine from Philadelphia, who I met after the war at Pompano Beach, FL, triggered a serious international incident. At the time, all the sailors in the Asiatic fleet were restricted to their ships. In order to supply the Peking legation, supplies came in from the northern province of Chinwantao, where the Great Wall of China came down to the sea. They had two Marines who rode shotgun on the supply train that went from Chinwantao to Peking. During the journey, they had to go through Tinsen, which was a Japanese-controlled territory. Normally, the train would travel through Tinsen without a problem.

This time, the Japanese stopped the train and wouldn't let them get ice for the goods that would spoil. They had to stay in Tinsen overnight. The Marine, a Corporal, was sitting in the boxcar next to his buddy, looking down on the dancing lights of the city. His buddy said, "I want to go down there and have a good time tonight." The Corporal let him go and told him he had to be back at such-and-such a time, so they could go on to Peking. At around two or three o'clock in the morning, a Japanese squad marched over to the train with his fellow Marine in custody. They approached the boxcar and the Japanese officer drew his samurai sword and swung it at his buddy, knocking off his hat. In the dark, the Marine Corporal thought the officer had cut his friend's head off. The Marine drew his .45 caliber pistol and shot all eight soldiers in the squad. He killed three of the Japanese soldiers and wounded the rest. Then, he took off.

For three days, the Japanese were hunting him down in Tinsen. At that time, we were restricted to the ship for a week due to the incident. We didn't know what was happening at the time. The rumors were that "a Marine went crazy'. I didn't find out all the details until years later in 1968 when I met the Marine, who was living in a condominium on the ocean at Pompano Beach, FL. I played golf with him several times and then he told me the story. I had also read a local newspaper article, which described the retired Marine capturing a robber in his condominium complex. Apparently, he did it with his .45 caliber pistol.

While the Japanese were trying to hunt him down in 1939, the Marine Corporal went to the British embassy legation in Tinsen. The British sent him away and didn't want anything to do with him. Normally, there are no Navy ships at Tinsen, but at this time, a destroyer had pulled into port. He swam out to the destroyer and was brought aboard. They arrested him and threw him in the brig. The Japanese wanted him to be turned over to them, but the U.S. Navy wouldn't do it. They kept him in the brig for six months with very little food. They gave him a General Court Martial and sent him back to the states. When he got back to the states, he was tried, convicted, and given a life sentence at Portsmouth. The Marine's family was very influential in Philadelphia and they were able to use their influence on the Mayor to get him out of prison and get him reinstated in the Marine Corps. During the war, he was the small arms instructor at Paris Island.

That year, 1939, a typhoon came through and we lost the *U.S.S Pigeon*, a submarine salvage vessel. She was high and dry on the rocks. The *Canopus* stayed behind to salvage it. It was no easy task. One month later, in late October, we departed and headed to Manila in the Philippines. *Pigeon* was saved. Shortly after anchoring in Manila Bay, six Navy P-boats {type of submarine} arrived from the states, bringing the sub fleet up to twelve; six old S-boats, six P-boats.

I settled in and was assigned to the refrigeration gang. There were eight of us. We ran our own liberty and fortunately, most were married men with their dependants back in the states. I was able to go ashore every night. I took up gambling on Jai-Alai which was very popular in the Orient. I figured out the system and made some money, which kept me going.

The name of the game was booze and sex. Naturally, there were women who worked the bars. If you wanted a woman for the night, you bought her out. You paid for her bar tab and bought her everything she wanted. There were all kinds of women in the bars. Some of them even followed the fleet up and down the coast.

Then, disaster struck three weeks after the stateside subs arrived. Many sailors on the P-boats came down with the clap {a Venereal Disease}. They had to be replaced. That was when I "volunteered" to work on the subs as a replacement. I did not do this on my own. I was drafted.

3

U.S.S. Permit

The first day of sub duty was very scary. We made 57 dives for training purposes. I was well aware of the *Squalus*, a sub that had sunk off Portsmouth, New Hampshire six months before. All diving procedures had been changed after that. The biggest change was the engine room stop valves were now closed permanently. The subs no longer depended on the main induction valve to close, which is why the *Squalus* sank during a malfunction.

Now, before any dive, all openings to the sea were closed manually, except the conning tower hatch, which was called taking suction through the boat. A gale blew through to the engine room, where four diesels required a lot of air instead of through the main induction. On long surface trips, the main induction was used.

My diving station was the stern planes, which regulated diving depth. Next, I had to learn all the other stations and how to operate them. This took six months. I was promoted to Fireman first class E-4 and received $10.00 sub pay and then $25.00 per month, when I was qualified after six months. I was now earning $85.00 per month. Wow! My last tour of mess cooking came up. I didn't mind it a bit. When in port, the first man up {for liberty} became the cook. It didn't matter who, officer or enlisted. I liked that. Everyone was equal.

We engaged in routine patrols, mostly in the China Sea near Japan. I never knew the exact location of the patrols. But, when a Jap destroyer nearly ran us down, I knew we were close. The diving depth was either 35 ft or 65 ft and the submerged speed was one or two knots.

Six of our subs went into Shanghai. They anchored at the Standard Oil docks about ten miles down the Wang-pu River. We had to have two men on the subs with boat hooks to push all the dead bodies in the water out of the way. The bodies of thousands of Chinese people, who died from starvation, floated in the river.

The Highlanders and the 4th Marine Regiment patrolled the International Settlement. They were the police force there. They told me they used to pick up

17

20,000 dead bodies every night. They were all Chinese people who had starved to death.

A bridge went from the International Settlement to the side that the Japanese controlled. There were Marines on one side of the bridge and Japanese soldiers on the other. People were allowed to go back and forth, but they had to have the right passes. I used to think it was a great place. It was the Paris of the Far East.

During a leave in Shanghai, I was sitting in a cabaret with some of my Navy buddies. We had a guy with us, who we used to call "Wobbly Jones", because he was half-drunk most of the time. We were sitting at a table having a few drinks, when we saw four Scotsmen sitting nearby. We got into a discussion about whether the Highlanders were wearing anything under their kilts. We elected Wobbly Jones to find out. We figured he would go over their table and ask them. Wobbly Jones went over to their table and lifted up one of the Scotsman's kilts to check underneath. The big Scotsman belted him one, knocking him down a flight of stairs.

When Wobbly came back to the table, we said, "Well, did he have anything on underneath?"

Wobbly replied, "I don't remember." There were some wild times in those days.

Summer 1940. We operated out of Tsingtao. The water there was shallow, yellow, and dirty. We always had company. The Jap destroyers were fast and big, compared to what we had at that time. All our torpedoes were armed and tubed. We carried sixteen torpedoes. Four were in the super-structure, six in tubes, and six in ready tracks on both torpedo rooms; four forward, two aft.

Our sub, the *U.S.S Permit S.S. 178*, was originally named the *Pinna*. All the equipment still had *Pinna* plates. The story goes that some little old lady contacted the Navy and told them that the *Pinna* was a fish that buried itself in the mud when it was scared. So, the Navy changed the sub's name to the *Permit*. The *Permit* was used to make the movie "D1", which came out in 1937. The movie was about a showboat built in New London in 1936. All other ships were built in Portsmouth, NH, a Naval shipyard.

The *Permit* could do 24 knots on the surface, which was considered fast in those days. The sub required constant care and the crew did everything. I learned a lot about machinery.

I was in the auxiliary gang for one stint, and I'll never forget when I received a jolt of electricity when I secured the main air compressor. The jolt knocked me out for about fifteen minutes.

My boss said, "Now, I'll show you how to do it."

But, from then on, I avoided it.

This was the year, 1940, when my mom died. The executive officer gave me ten dollars and four days on the beach. I never got over this.

My, how time was passing me by. I thought my time in the Navy was a waste of time, but then I figured I had a little over a year to go and I could stand on my head for the rest of my hitch.

I lived with a gal named Pat Schuller. She said she was half Canuck {Hawaiian} and half American soldier. A great gal. I'll never forget, while dining out, I saw her with Lieutenant {Moon} Chapple, who was an engineer officer on the *U.S.S. Perch*. The *U.S.S. Perch* was normally out to sea while we were in port. To his amazement, she came over to me and threw her arms around me. The next day back on the ship, I was ordered to sick bay on the *Canopus* for a standard short arm inspection. I always wondered why. Apparently, Lt. Chapple ordered the medical inspection to find out if I had any social diseases.

Lt. Chapple got his nickname, "Moon", from his days at the Naval Academy. Every time he walked by the statue of the famous Indian warrior, Tecumseh, he used to drop his pants and "moon" the statue. He got all kinds of demerits for it. Chapple was a big guy, a college heavyweight boxing champ. We also used to call him "Snowshoes" because he was a sloppy guy whose clothes never seemed to fit him.

One time, the subs *U.S.S Permit* and *U.S.S Tarpon* were in dry-dock at "the Dewey" in Subic Bay. At that time, Lt. Chapple was the engineering officer on the *Tarpon*. There was a bar nearby called the "Green Room", which served the coldest beer in the Philippines. Some of the guys on the base used to sneak over there and drink beers when they were supposed to be working.

Lt. Chapple came up to the bar one day and told the guys to "get back to work".

A big boatswain mate said to him, "If you take them two stripes off your shoulder, I'll knock your ass off."

Chapple took off the stripes, they went outside, and Chapple whipped the shit out of him. Lt. Chapple was "a Prince". A regular officer {a prick} would have just put the guys on report.

Lt. Chapple was promoted to the Skipper of the *S-37*, which was the only sub opposing the Japanese in the Philippines at the outbreak of the war. Chapple received the Navy Cross for sinking three Japanese ships when he was commanding the submarine *S-37*. Chapple was later in command of the *U.S.S. Permit*, one of the only two submarines that ever reached the Sea of Japan. The only way they could get in was through the Straits of Tsushima, which was between Korea and the southern tip of Japan, about fifty miles wide. The Japanese had the area heavily mined. They made it through to the Sea of Japan by following a ship in. He wrote that it was like there was no war going on there. All the cities on the west coast of Japan had all their lights on. All the ships in the Sea of Japan were also lit up. They had a field day there. They sank a whole bunch of ships and then got out. He retired a Rear Admiral. The *Permit* survived World War II with a great record.

By the end of World War II, American submarines sank 45% of the Japanese Navy and 65% of the Japanese merchant ships. Our fleet of submarines crippled Japan. The Japanese didn't sail their ships in convoys. A convoy was when a group of ships moved in a zig-zag motion, making them difficult targets to hit. The Japanese ships used to travel single-file along the China coast. They were easy pickings for our submarines. We lost fifty-four submarines in World War II out of a fleet of approximately 250 at the end of the war. Some of them never even got into action. Our submarines could go 25 knots and get ahead of most of the convoys.

I expected to return to the U.S. in June, 1941, but the Navy held all sub sailors over for one year. It was all in the Shipping Articles. The Navy was letting other guys out six months early. All qualified submariners were held over. We were the only ones held over for an extra year. That did it.

June, 1941. I was transferred to Olongapo in the Philippines. It was about sixty miles north of Manila, where the Navy had a floating dry-dock called "the Dewey". The Navy had a battery overhaul unit stationed there, which was staffed by 80 men and a Chief Warrant in charge.

All batteries were being changed because they were five years old. War was coming and the subs were getting ready. It took about one month to do one sub.

It was Rainy Season and they measured the rainfall there in feet. It rained all the time. Four of us bought a 1929 model A Ford, which we used to go to Manila on weekends. We paid $50.00 for it. There was an aviation unit station near us, so we had all the gas we needed. There were drums of gas all over the place. How nice. We were not allowed off the Naval reservation, but you know how rules are meant to be broken. This was hard work, but I managed to get off weekends {72hours} plus. I think the 29 Ford saved my life later. All of us hung out at Yat-wa's, which was a Chinese store with a bar. We checked our booze behind the bar and carefully marked it. To become a member of the battery over-haul club, you had to drink a sip of everything behind the bar, ending up with a shaker nearly full of booze. Then, you had to get up off the barstool and walk away. While we were there for five months, no one walked. Believe me.

The base at Olongapo had a platoon of Marines, who acted as police for the town and reservation. The base commander was a Reserve Lt., U.S. Navy. It was a small base with 150 sub sailors and about 200 flyboys. It was quite crowded. We had a base bar that served beer only. The bar was 40 feet long and a stretched python skin was hanging on the wall behind it. We called the bar the Tin Roof. They served the coldest beer I ever had.

November 29th, 1941. I am sent down to Manila for supplies. While I'm at the Caviti Navy yard, I see A.A. {anti-aircraft} guns being hastily loaded onto the Houston, our heavy cruiser.

I go up to one of the sailors on the dock and ask him. "What the hell's going on?"

"Haven't you heard?" He asked.

"Heard what?"

"The Japs are about to attack us!"

It turns out there is a Condition Three Alert and all leave is canceled.

I fly back to Olongapo in a PBY {reconnaissance seaplane} with supplies that afternoon. I find out they never got word of the alert. A Condition Three Alert basically means you can expect to be attacked at any minute.

The reason for the Condition Three Alert was because our radio operators had lost all contact with the Japanese fleet. Every Naval Code-man stationed in the Philippines was responsible for monitoring a particular Japanese ship in their fleet. On November 29th, 1941, every ship in the main Japanese battle fleet stopped broadcasting on their radios. They were on radio silence. Of course, the reason for their radio silence was because they were on their way to Pearl Harbor. It is interesting that the Asiatic fleet knew about the imminent threat of a Japanese attack, but Pearl Harbor didn't. Was our communication network so poor that we couldn't get a message from the Philippines to Hawaii? Why wasn't Pearl Harbor placed on a Condition Three Alert when the Japanese fleet went into radio silence? The reason was that Pearl Harbor was a setup. Everyone I knew in the Navy believed Pearl Harbor was intentionally set up by FDR and other military brass to get us into the European War.

The next day, November 30th, 1941, a PBY seaplane comes into base all shot up. It has to run up on the ramp to keep from sinking. I have a buddy in the crew and he's the only one hit. He's bleeding very badly, but he can walk. I meet him an hour later and he shows me his wound. A piece of aluminum from the hull took most of his foreskin off. I think that may have been the first wound of World War II. I wonder if it was ever recorded as such.

The PBYs were flying over the Jap fleet, where their troops were landing in Indo-China, eight days before Pearl Harbor. All stops were off to get two subs back to sea. I got to go to Manila one more time during the weekend before World War II broke out.

Coming back from Manila in our 1929 Ford, a dam broke, flooding the valley with three feet of water for eight miles. With the help of some local Filipinos, we are able to push the car to higher ground. By the time we get back, it's 11:00am; two hours over leave, so technically A.W.O.L. {Absent With-Out Leave}.

We are attached temporarily to the U.S.S. Shark. The Skipper's name is Lt. Dempsey. He throws us in the brig for ten days plus piss and punk {bread and water}.

The Marine guard informs us, "Don't worry. You'll get a full ration. We don't like that son-of-a-bitch, Dempsey."

Three days later, they let us out. We go back to work. Then, Lt. Dempsey has the nerve to ask us to ship out on the Shark-SS175. I tell him I would never serve under him. Forty-two days later after the war broke out, the Shark-SS175 was lost, all hands gone. I guess my luck had changed.

4

Ambush

December 8^{th,} 1941. Olongapo, Philippines.

04:00 Everybody is turned out of their bunks and told that the Japs had bombed Pearl Harbor. Not having been assigned a battle station, I just shrug my shoulders and roll over. I figure it is just another drill, not realizing it's the real McCoy.

06:00 A Manila news broadcast wakes me up and I realize that it's not just a dream. For the past three months, I've sweated out a transport, and now that I had almost realized my dream, them bastards have to upset my playhouse. Oh well, that's life for you.

All of us are shaken out of the sack and issued rifles and ammunition, 100 rounds each. It was definite. The Japs had bombed Pearl Harbor. Three-hundred-fifty Japanese torpedo bombers, dive-bombers, and fighters had achieved complete surprise when they hit the American fleet at Pearl Harbor shortly before 8:00am on December 7th, 1941 {Hawaiian time, which is December 8th Pacific time-our time}. They attacked our airfields on the Hawaiian island of Oahu at the same time they hit our ships. They needed to destroy the American fighter planes, so they couldn't take off to intercept their bombers. Most of our planes were hit before they could take off. We lost 188 planes and 159 were damaged.

The main target of the Japanese bombers were the seven battleships anchored in an area called "Battleship Row", which was located along the southeast shore of Ford Island. The battleship *U.S.S Pennsylvania* was in a dry-dock on the other side of the channel. All the ships in Battleship Row were hit with bombs and torpedoes during the first wave of the attack. The battleships *U.S.S. West Virginia* and the *U.S.S. Oklahoma* were both sunk in the first wave. The battleship *U.S.S Arizona* was hit with an armor-piercing bomb, causing catastrophic explosions when it ignited the forward ammunition magazines. The explosions and fire on the *Arizona* killed more than a thousand crewmen, which was about half of the total Americans killed during the entire attack. The other ships in Battleship

Row, the *U.S.S. Maryland, U.S.S. Nevada, U.S.S. California,* and *U.S.S. Tennessee* were all severely damaged in the first wave of the attack.

The *U.S.S. Nevada* attempted to escape, despite the serious damage inflicted on her during the first wave. The second wave of attack planes arrived and started bombing the *Nevada* as she got underway in the channel. The Japanese were attempting to block the narrow entrance to the harbor by trying to sink the *Nevada*. The *Nevada* was ordered to beach, so the channel would remain clear.

When the attack ended at 9:45am, 2,335 servicemen and 68 civilians had been killed, with 1,178 wounded. Three of our battleships had been severely damaged and five had been sunk. We also lost three destroyers and three light cruisers. The Japanese only lost 27 planes and five midget submarines. Three of the U.S. Pacific fleet aircraft carriers, *Enterprise, Lexington,* and *Saratoga,* had been ordered away from Pearl Harbor previously to December 7th {Hawaiian time}. The American aircraft carriers, which had been the prime targets of the Japanese attack, were all unharmed.

Now we settle down to wartime routine. No more liberty, no pretty gals, no place to drown one's sorrows, or just drown. The job I'm working on requires day and night work with only a cat-nap once in a while. The 4th Marines, 1000 of them, have been with us one week, so the base is crowded now. They had come down from Shanghai, China on December 1st.

December 8th, 1941. Approximately 12:15 pm {Pacific time-about nine hours after the initial bombing at Pearl Harbor}. A catastrophic attack was launched by Japanese bombers against our two main airfields in the Philippines; the Clark Airfield and Iba Airfield. The Clark Airfield was the base for seventeen B-17 bombers, 18 P-40E fighter planes, and 18 P-40B fighter planes. Most of the planes were caught on the ground during the "surprise" air attack. I say surprise with quotes because this foreseeable attack occurred only nine hours after the surprise attack on Pearl Harbor. It is baffling that, after experiencing Pearl Harbor, we were still not ready for a Japanese air attack and we were "surprised" for a second time only nine hours later.

As the bombs fell, the American forces tried to launch some of their P-40 fighter planes. Most of the American planes were either blown up, while they were taking off, by Japanese bombers or destroyed in low-altitude strafing attacks by Japanese fighters. Only four P-40s were able to get into the air to engage the enemy aircrafts. American pilot, Randall B. Keator, shot down the first Japanese aircraft over the Philippines. Another American aviator, Lt. Moore, was able to destroy two more Japanese planes during vicious aerial dogfights. A small group of aviators in nearby Del Carmen Field saw the smoke rising from Clark Field and took off in their P-35s to assist the vastly outnumbered P-40s. Despite being outmaneuvered by the technically superior Japanese planes, the P-35s from Del Carmen were able to destroy three more Japanese planes. `

The small group of American planes was far too outnumbered to stop the tide of destruction unleashed on Clark Airfield. Sixteen out of the fleet of seventeen B-17 bombers were destroyed on the ground. The only B-17 to survive was the one piloted by Lt. John Carpenter, which had been flying a reconnaissance mission over the Japanese airfields at Formosa, in preparation for an attack. The massive destruction at Clark Airfield stopped the Americans' planned attack from ever happening. Only a handful of the P-40 fighter planes from the airfield survived the attack. Most were destroyed on the ground or taking off.

At about the same time as the attack on Clark, Japanese bombers and fighters were racing toward our second major airfield in the Philippines; Iba Airfield. A squad of P-40 planes was just returning to Iba Airfield after a long-range reconnaissance, when the Japanese bombers and fighters attacked the airfield. The returning American fighters engaged the enemy aircraft and were able to prevent the low-level strafing that had caused so much damage at Clark Field. The returning American planes had been low on fuel, so three of them were forced to crash-land on the beach when their fuel gave out. Five others were shot down in aerial dogfights. Some of the courageous ground and combat crews were able to man the machine gun turrets on the grounded planes and fire back at the Japanese bombers and fighters. Other heroic American soldiers stood by their AA guns, while they were being relentlessly strafed by enemy fighters. Only two American P-40 fighter planes survived the attack.

There is much controversy concerning the reasons why our two major airfields in the Philippines were caught completely unprepared. Why were the two American airfields sitting ducks for the attacking Japanese air force, when only nine hours earlier Pearl Harbor had been caught in a similar surprise air attack?

Poor communication played its role in the destruction of the airfields. The radar station at Nichols Field allegedly sent a warning to Clark Field about a large formation of enemy aircraft flying south over northern Luzon. The Chief of the Aircraft Warning Service at Nichols, Col. A.H. Campbell, insists that a warning had been sent and acknowledged by Clark Field. General Eubank at Clark Field insists that Bomber Command never received a warning from Nichols.

Another controversy concerning the destruction of the airfields relates to the military's bureaucratic chain-of-command. The air force commander in charge of Clark Airfield, General Brereton, and the commander of all the armed forces in the Philippines, General MacArthur, have told conflicting accounts of what happened directly before the attacks on the airfields. At about 5am on December 8th, 1941, General Brereton said he reported to General MacArthur's headquarters at Fort Santiago to request permission to attack the Japanese airfields at Formosa. Brereton said he met with MacArthur's Chief of Staff, Brig. General Richard K. Sutherland, and Sutherland said he would pass his request on to General Mac-Arthur. MacArthur later said he didn't know anything about the request. Brereton said he continued to make requests for the rest of the morning and General Sutherland told him he was only authorized to take "defensive action", but no "offensive action" against the Japanese airfields at Formosa.

Brereton said he returned to Clark airfield and continued to call Sutherland at Fort Santiago, making requests to take offensive action. Records at Clark corroborate his story. After making numerous calls to Sutherland, Brereton said Sutherland finally authorized a reconnaissance mission to Formosa to spy on the enemy airfields in preparation for an attack. Brereton said he was explicitly told by Sutherland not to take any offensive action against the Japanese airfields on Formosa until after a reconnaissance mission had been completed. While we were launching our recon mission, the Japanese were launching their second "surprise" attack. The B-17 that was sent on the recon mission to Formosa was the only one that survived the attack on Clark Airfield. The rest of the grounded B-17s were destroyed in the attack. Official records indicate that MacArthur stayed in seclusion during the morning of December 8th and communicated with his generals via his Chief of Staff, General Sutherland. It seems highly unusual that General MacArthur did not directly communicate with his generals to talk about war strategy directly after the Pearl Harbor surprise attack. The controversy concerning whether Brereton made continuous requests to attack Formosa and was told not to attack by MacArthur's Chief of Staff, Sutherland, continues to this day.

December 9th, 1941. Seven American PBYs {reconnaissance seaplanes} landed at our base in Olongapo and are anchored out in the bay. At about 10:00am, two TYBF's {Jap fighter planes} come skimming over the water toward the PBY's, firing their machine guns. We were warned and we are waiting for them. Three hundred sailors with rifles and four to five hundred Marines fire at these planes. The Jap fighter planes set all seven PBYs on fire and fly off. No loss of life. Years later, I found out the planes crashed in the jungle. It was too bad we didn't know that then. If we had known where they had crashed at the time, our engineers could have studied them for weaknesses.

December 10th, 1941. We found out the Caviti Navy Yard had been destroyed by a Japanese air raid. Apparently, the A.A. guns at the Cavite Yard had a range of 15,000 feet, while the Japanese bombers attacked the yard from

23,000 feet, rendering the anti-aircraft fire completely ineffective. The Marines defending the base had been told to fire small arms at strafing planes, but the surrounding buildings limited their field of fire. The hospital in the Navy Yard received a direct hit, so a temporary first aid station was set up in the Marines' library in the barracks. At the time, everyone thought the targeting of hospitals in the air raid was the result of an accidental bombing, because the rules of western warfare prohibited the intentional targeting of hospitals. Later in the war, it was learned that the direct targeting of hospitals was a conscious strategy used by the Japanese, which was implemented to cause maximum casualties. Fires were burning all over the base, so the Marines improvised firefighting units. They joined with Filipino firefighters to put out all the blazes. About a thousand civilians were killed in the attack and five hundred wounded were treated at the improvised first aid station.

Two subs in the Cavite Navy Yard were hit and one was destroyed. The submarine, *Sea Dragon*, was badly damaged by a close hit, while the submarine, *Sea Lion*, was completely destroyed by a direct hit.

An American Navy sailor and future POW survivor, Hank Henderson, was standing on the dock at the Cavite Navy Yard during the bombing attack on December 10th, 1941. Mr. Henderson was assigned to the submarine tender, *U.S.S. Otus AS-20*, which was anchored at the Cavite Navy yard during the bombing raid. He wrote his own account of the attack:

> Fifty four Japanese Air Force heavy bombers made bombing runs over the Navy Yard at Cavite, completely destroying all facilities. I went out on the dock from the *U.S.S. Otus AS-20* with the Commander of Sub-Div 203 so he could give orders to the Commanders of the *U.S.S. Sea Lion SS-194* and the *U.S.S. Sea Dragon SS-193* to get under way and make preparations for starting war patrols against all Japanese vessels. As he was giving these orders, a bomb landed on the *USS Sea Lion SS-194*, rendering it useless as a combat vessel. How he and I were spared being hit by fragments of this bomb in particular, or for that matter, how we escaped without injury by any of the hundreds of bombs that rained down on this small US Navy Repair Facility is only known to God. {Henry Clay Henderson, U.S.N., "The Diary of Henry Clay Henderson", 1998, PT 1, p.1}

Hank Henderson was an expert spare-parts technician on the *U.S.S. Otus*. On December 12th, Mr. Henderson was sent back to the bombed-out Cavite Navy

Yard to salvage for torpedoes and submarine spare parts. He wrote the following account of his return to the Navy Yard:

> December 12ᵗʰ, 1941. Fri. Morning. I went to the Cavite Navy Yard to try to salvage any submarine spare parts or torpedoes. GOD what a sight. Dead bodies everywhere. Dogs, cats, chickens, and pigs were eating the flesh of these bodies. It was a scramble to find a place to put my foot down without stepping on someone or some dismembered part of a body. {Henderson, PT 1, p.2}

December 13ᵗʰ, 1941. We abandon the base, leaving the Marines to destroy it. We leave Olongapo in school buses and take two days to reach Manila. Everywhere we go, we meet Filipino soldiers who greet us with confident smiles. Way down deep I know we are only stalling for time. We don't stand a chance unless help arrives.

5

Mama San

The only remaining U.S. Navy ship in Manila Bay is my old ship, the *Canopus*. The rest of the U.S. Navy fleet has fled south to Australia. The *Canopus* is a submarine tender and she was left behind because two of our subs were hit. One of them was sunk, while one of them was salvageable. The *Canopus* stayed behind to repair it. Back aboard the good ole Mama-san, and boy am I glad I didn't get stuck on land to fight. That's no good.

My counterpart on the submarine tender *U.S.S. Otus* and future POW survivor, Hank Henderson, wrote his own account of the status of the *Otus* and the *Canopus* in his diary:

> The *U.S.S Otus* AS-20 got underway for Port Darwin, Australia. The Commander of the Sub-Div 203 gave me orders to commandeer a small motor launch and take us across Manila Bay to the *USS Holland*. He conferred with the Commander of Submarines Asiatic, Captain John Wilkes. Orders were issued for the *USS Holland* to proceed to Port Darwin, Australia. The Submarine Tender *USS Canopus* was ordered to remain behind and service the *USS Sea Dragon*, making it seaworthy for the Voyage to Australia. The *USS Sea Lion* was towed out to sea and sunk. I remained in the Port Area of Manila working with submarine spare parts, doing what I could to service the US submarines, helping to make them ready for war patrols. Some of these submarines intercepted the Japanese landing in Lingayen Gulf in Northern Luzon. {Henderson, PT 1 p.1}

Mr. Henderson confirms the fact that the *USS Canopus* was the only submarine tender left behind in the Philippines. Like me, he also remained behind to keep our submarine fleet going.

The Captain of the *Canopus*, Commander Sackett, described the status of the ship and it's mission, while it was docked in the port area of Manila;

> The superstructure of the *Canopus* was painted to match the color of the docks alongside, and camouflage nets were spread overhead in an effort to deceive the Japs as long as possible as to our identity. The more exposed fuel tanks were emptied and filled with water to reduce the danger of a disastrous fire, which might make it impossible to save the ship if the oil were touched off by a bomb. With the ship as ready as the men could make her, the grim question as to whether the value of her services in the time left to her would be worth the expected sacrifice was all that remained to be decided. {Sackett, p.8}

The crews aboard the *Canopus* repair the submarine, *Sea Dragon*, so it is fit to operate. The *Sea Dragon* leaves the Philippines on December 14th to join the rest of the fleet down south. The *Canopus* also repairs three minesweepers, three gun-boats, and engages in ship {*The Pigeon*} and sub salvages. We could make a run for it, but I guess we're too slow. I'll never know.

December 15th, 1941. I'm now assigned to the Oil King Gang. Our job is to obtain and protect the limited precious oil supply that exists. I had been part of this group before for a short period of time. I knew all five guys in the group.

December 16th, 1941. Big day for the *Canopus*. We are sitting on the bottom between piers one and three, acting as anti-aircraft protection. Most of our oil is pumped out to hidden tanks ashore. We take on water ballasts. We're equipped with four 3-inch AA-guns shielded with 2-inch boilerplates.

Here they come. Fifty-four Betty's {Japanese bombers} flying in formation heading right for us, and the port area of Manila. Noontime. About a mile from us, they hit the Navy Club and many cheers go up from the crew. I'll tell about that later. We take shelter below decks. Why? We are told to do it. The bombs begin to hit all around us and some actually hit us. The explosions are deafening and we feel helpless.

In the middle of the chaos, my friend turns to me and says, "We're finished. We're not getting out of this alive."

I look him straight in the eye and say, "Don't worry. She's a tough ship. Good Ol' Mama-san will hold together. There's nothing to worry about."

I was lying.

All members of the AA battery, 36 men, are hit with shrapnel, but none are killed. We go around plugging up holes in the side of the ship with wood plugs.

Later, I go up to see the damage. The thing that I can't believe is the shrapnel holes in the AA guns' 2" boiler plates, as if a welding torch did it.

The reason the cheers went up when the Navy Club was hit was because the enlisted men of the Asiatic fleet paid for the club through a forced collection prior to the war. On opening night, some drunken sailors threw Admiral Hart into the wading pool, not knowing who he was. Apparently, he was interfering with their fun. The next day, the club became Shore Patrol Headquarters, and enlisted men were restricted, as the previous agreement was no officers and no Shore Patrol. All this was gone. Ten years earlier, the same thing happened at the Army and Navy Club. The enlisted men of the fleet paid for the club with their contributions. Then, the officers took over and no enlisted men were allowed.

About a week later, I have to work guard duty. We are told there is the possibility that Japanese skin divers will come in and place explosives on the ship. We are supposed to patrol back and forth on the dock. Another guard patrols one section of dock and I patrol the other. I say to him, "I don't know what you're going to do, but I'm not going to stomp up and down all night. I'm going to find a cubby-hole somewhere where I can sit there and get some rest. If someone comes by and doesn't respond, I'll just shoot them."

We carry rifles with fixed bayonets and keep the safety's off. I'm resting in my cubby-hole when I hear someone approaching in the dark. I don't say anything at first. I corner him with my bayonet.

Then, I say, "Who the hell are you?"

He answers, "I'm Captain Sackett."

I look him up and down and say, "Okay, you can pass."

He saves a lot of us by getting us off the ship during the air attacks. He's all right.

Captain Sackett was a good guy, but most of the enlisted men liked the guy before him even better. The Skipper before him was Captain Bannerman and he was an old drunk. Every time we went to the Navy Club in Tsingtao, if he was there, he always sent over a round of drinks to us. That was very unusual at the time. Usually, officers had nothing to do with enlisted men.

In 1939, I got sent back to the ship once for slapping a girl, while I was in a bar in Tsingtao. It was early Sunday morning. We had got into an argument, so I slapped her in the face. It was the only time in my life I did something like that. This guy came walking by wearing a "pith helmet", which we used to call a "Frank Buck helmet", which meant he was an MP {Military Police}. He had a walking stick in his hand and he wore Bermuda shorts with high socks.

He said to me, "Son, you shouldn't treat a woman like that."

I said, "Who the hell are you?"

He said, "I'm Captain Carroll, Chief of Staff, Asiatic Fleet."

So I said, "Why don't you take the four stripes out of your ass and put them on your shoulder where they belong?"

Then I ran out of the bar, jumped into a rickshaw, and took off.

He blew a whistle and suddenly I had the Shore Patrol all around me. They picked me up and sent me back to the ship. I was under Shore Patrol arrest. I had to go to mast, but I missed Exec Mast, so they held me over for Captain's Mast. Captain Bannerman was presiding.

He looked at the Shore Patrol report and asked, "Did you really say that to Captain Carroll? I want you to repeat what you said to him."

I repeated it. He broke out laughing so hard, he almost fell down.

He said, "Two days deprivation of liberty."

This meant nothing to me because we went ashore whenever we wanted to.

Captain Bannerman's tour was eventually up. Captain Sackett replaced him. Commander Sackett had a lot to do with submarine engineering. He was instrumental in salvaging the *Squalus*, which sank off of Portsmouth, NH in 1939.

Working in the Oil King Gang, I know the status of the oil on board—there is very little. But the plan is if we are to move, we can take our oil back and fill up our tanks. Oil and water don't mix, which we find out later.

Captain Sackett decides that as long as our AA guns are falling short, all hands will seek shelter ashore when the air raid alarm goes off. That's all we need. We find a nice bar and grill two blocks from the ship, right next to the slit trenches we're supposed to use as cover. The bar is a cabaret-type place called the "Black Cat", where there's five or six cabaret girls and all the booze you want. A retired Army Sergeant runs the bar. Everyday bombs hit close by. They are some hits! It's like drinking with an unrelenting thunderstorm perpetually exploding in the background.

December 21st, 1941. The American submarine, *Stingray*, spots a Japanese invasion fleet at Lingayen Gulf, which is on the northwest shore of the main Philippines Island of Luzon. Manila is only one hundred miles to the south. Admiral Hart sends four submarines to join *Stingray* in the fight. The American submarines attack, but are unable to sink the approaching Japanese transports due to shallow water and faulty torpedoes. The only exception is the *S-38* submarine commanded by Lieutenant "Moon" Chapple. Chapple makes the only confirmed kill by sinking the 5,500-ton Japanese troop transport, *Hayo Maru*.

December 22nd, 1941. The Japanese invasion force overpowers resistance and establishes a beachhead on the shores of Lingayen Gulf. A single Filipino battalion defends the area gallantly, but they are overwhelmed by the Japanese forces' sheer numbers. The Japanese 48th Division and 14th Army, consisting of 35,000 ground troops, begin to fight its way south.

Apparently, General MacArthur miscalculated when he set up the beach defenses. MacArthur had placed the bulk of the Fil-American artillery forty miles south of the area where the Japanese landed.

December 23rd, 1941. The Japanese 16th Division, consisting of 7000 ground troops, land at Lamon Bay, 200 miles southeast of Lingayen Gulf. They overpower resistance and begin fighting their way toward Manila.

December 24th, 1941. No sooner do I sit down to dinner, when the air raid siren goes off. There have been so many mistakes made in the Manila signals, so we're not supposed to pay any attention to them. We're supposed to wait until the siren is sounded aboard the ship. There it goes and away I go! Only the AA crew and some black gang stay aboard. The rest of us seek shelter ashore, but it gives us a good excuse to go over and have a few cold ones. Well, here I am having a nice cold one in the proper atmosphere {our favorite local bar, "The Black Cat"}, when the front window shatters, tables blow over, and everybody hits the deck. Things quiet down and we rush outside to see what the score is. There's a bomb crater right in front of the joint. The port area is burning in many spots.

The retired Army Sergeant, who owns the bar, tells us, "I'm heading for the hills. You guys help yourself."

That was the end of the good times.

It looks like old Mama-san, the *Canopus,* has taken it on the chin. So we go back to the ship and find out they dropped bombs all around her, but there were no direct hits. That night on December 24th, our ship started to take on oil to prepare for departure. When we leave, Manila is going to be an open city with no defense.

Despite heavy fighting, the massive Japanese invasion force continues its relentless advance toward Manila. General MacArthur has ordered all Fil-American forces to evacuate to the Bataan peninsula. Our forces on the front lines are falling back to defensive positions and attempting to delay the Japanese advance, hoping it will give us time to evacuate all our sailors, soldiers, and supplies to Bataan. All of our armaments and materials are being moved south into Bataan or blown up.

The city of Manila is surrounded by fire from all the demolition going on. Close to a million gallons of oil have been ignited. The marine railway, ammunition depot, and Sangley Point radio station have been blown up with dynamite and depth charges. Secret documents and files are being destroyed everywhere. Everything that may be of any value to the Japanese is being obliterated.

Commander Sackett described the situation in Manila in his own narrative.

> There was every indication that conditions would get no better, and with the Army falling back on Manila, word came that the city would soon be abandoned to avoid complete destruction. Although the *Canopus* was still intact, the harbor could no longer be used for a submarine base. The circle of bombing attacks was drawing tighter each day, and on Christmas Eve our headquarters was hit, and spent bomb fragments landed on our decks.
>
> During the night we got underway for what proved to be our last journey, and steamed out of the Bay toward Corregidor, with great fires and towering columns of smoke astern of us as evidence that the Army was scorching the earth as they prepared to withdraw into Bataan. {Sackett, p.10}

We are preparing the ship for getting underway. Boy, I hope we join the rest of the fleet down south, but I doubt it because I've already been told the inside dope on how much fuel we have and how far it will take us.

6

Battleground: Bataan

It is dark and we are underway in Manila Bay. I take a trip up topside for air and I realize something disastrous is taking place in Manila. The sky is red and heavy. Explosions are going off continuously in that direction.

We take on as much oil as we can and get underway. We have to go through Navy mine fields, which contain contact mines. That night, we lose the fire in the boilers twice because of water in the oil. If the ship remains dead in the water, we could drift into one of the mines. We have to hand feed the boilers. We form a "bucket brigade", which hands off buckets of diesel oil from man-to-man, so we can keep the boilers firing. Luckily, we avoid the mines and arrive at Mariveles Bay, which is on the southern tip of the Bataan peninsula. The bay is about two miles in diameter with an opening about three or four hundred yards wide. We cover the ship with fishnets and tree branches to hide it from air attack. This would be the last place the *Canopus* would stay before we were forced to sink her.

Commander Sackett described the strategic importance of the move to Mariveles Bay;

> It was hoped that Mariveles Bay, being close to the guns of Corregidor, would be immune to air attacks, although some misgivings were felt on that score when we found a bombed and burning merchant ship in the harbor, and learned that this was the result of a light hearted Japanese Christmas Eve celebration. However, with high hopes, we moored the ship to the shoreline in a protected cove, and again spread out camouflage nets overhead. This time, the object was to make the ship look like part of the jungle foliage ashore, and we succeeded very well by using mottled green paint, with plenty of tree branches tied to the masts and upper works. Unfortunately, a rock quarry nearby had made a white gash in the cliff, and from one direction, this made a background which it was impossible to match. We could only hope the Jap scouting planes would not happen to snap any candid camera shots from that particular direction. {Sackett, p.11}

We are still fully operational. All shops are at 100%. We have time to fix anything mechanical, which we proceed to do. We are able to service jobs until late February, 1942. We service PT boats and all kinds of small crafts patrolling the Bataan defense area.

The Bataan peninsula is twenty-five miles long and twenty miles at its widest point. A series of high volcanic peaks are scattered throughout the jungle landscape. The east coast of the Bataan peninsula connects with Manila Bay, while the rocky west coast borders the China Sea. Mariveles Bay is located on the southern tip of the peninsula. The interior jungles of Bataan are so dense that visibility is limited to ten yards in any direction. Wild boars and chickens live in the jungle undergrowth. Forty-foot pythons slither through the underbrush in search of prey. On many areas of the coast, high cliffs drop down to the ocean far below. Beyond the cliffs, pinnacles of rock thrust up from the water like jagged, reaching tentacles.

By early January, 1942, we have 80,000 American and Filipino troops dug-in to defensive positions on the Bataan peninsula. More than half of our troops are fighting against the Japanese army on the front lines. General Wainwright is in charge of all the troops on the west side of the line, while General Parker commands the troops on the east side. The Japanese army has a major advantage over our forces because they control the air and sea.

On the nearby shore of Mariveles Bay, there is a rock-crushing complex, where they make aggregate to build roads. We use this as our ship's headquarters on Bataan. About a half-mile up the road, the Army engineers have dug immense tunnels into the side of the mountain. These tunnels serve as the Navy Headquarters on Bataan. All our records are kept there. If you travel further down the road along Mariveles Bay, you reach two more tunnels. One tunnel is filled with aerial bombs and the other is filled with gasoline.

The Mariveles Section Base is located to the northwest, which houses Army soldiers, mining engineers, radar operators, and medical personnel. The Section Base in Mariveles is protected by Anti-Aircraft Batteries A and C. Battery A is located high on the mountainside ridges, which are used as lookout points. From there, they can overlook most of the harbor area. Battery C is located in a dried-out rice paddy surrounded by sandbags. Many residents of the Section Base are bivouacked in the jungle because of the constant threat of air raids.

The rocky island of Corregidor is visible in the distance {two miles away} if you gaze across Mariveles Bay toward the ocean. A minefield separates the island from the bay. Travel between Mariveles Bay and Corregidor is only possible if a navigator knows the exact positions of the mines. Corregidor is the most heavily-fortified and well-defended American position in the Philippines. Numerous mortar cannons, machine guns, and Anti-Aircraft guns are positioned in trenches all over the rocky island. Corregidor is about three and a half miles long and one and a half miles at its widest point. The island is shaped like a giant pollywog. The highest position on the island {Malinta Hill} is located about halfway down its length and tapers off into the "tail", which is known as Hooker Point.

Corregidor is known as "the Rock", which is an appropriate name for the heavily-defended fortress-island. The north shore of the Rock faces Bataan, while the south shore is opposite Cavite. Some of the big guns on Corregidor can reach all the way to Bataan and Cavite. Corregidor's fourteen-inch guns use shells weighing 1,500 pounds and require over 400 pounds of explosive powder. General MacArthur's headquarters has been moved from Manila to Corregidor's Malinta Tunnel; an 800-foot long, fifty-foot wide tunnel, which the Army engineers blasted through the center of Malinta Hill with dynamite and then dug out with heavy machinery. There is also a separate tunnel containing the Navy Radio Intercept Tunnel known as "Station Cast", where American code-breakers monitor transmissions from the Japanese fleet.

December 25th, 1941. Yeah, today is Christmas, and here we are in Mariveles Bay, tied up to a makeshift dock. Why? Because we are too big and slow to make a run for it, so we have to stay here and let the Japs use us for bombing practice. Oh well, that's the breaks.

December 29th, 1941. We thought we were pretty well camouflaged. That is, up until today. A group of high altitude bombers fly over and drop the mail around old Mama-San. They pattern bomb us. Most of the bombs miss us, but the explosions still sound very close. Only one of the 500-pound bombs hits its mark. That's all it takes. The armor-piercing projectile plunges through the three decks aft and explodes on the propeller shaft in the shaft alley. The force of the explosion blasts upward and kills one man, a friend named Rex. The shaft alley sends the main force of the explosion into the engine room. This is where the engine room crew and fire room crew have taken shelter. Five out of ten men are killed and four are wounded. Only the Chief Petty Officer is uninjured. A sailor named "Bull Shantz" carries away nearly all the injured sailors from the engine room.

I am lucky. I had taken shelter ashore when the bomb hit. My boss, Squire Boon Zane, who took the place where I was usually assigned, was killed. There are four of us under an overhang of rock on the beach about a half-mile from the ship. The bombs exploded all around us. The one that hits close is ten feet directly above us. I thought we had it, but when the smoke cleared, we were shaken but okay. We run back to the ship to help put out the fires and bury the dead that night at sea. I am in the burial party, as I know all the men who were killed. As we are committing one at a time to the deep and after counting six splashes, we hear a seventh splash.

It's pitch black out and talk about being scared. We fish out one of the party from the water; his name is Earl LaFrance. He's alive. It's like a scene in a Hollywood movie.

Commander Sackett described the attack that day from his perspective;

> On December 29th, our daily visitors, evidently deciding that Manila had been adequately taken care of, turned their attention toward us. Squadron after endless squadron showed their contempt for the guns of Corregidor by blasting that island from end to end, and the last group of the day, as if by an afterthought, wheeled in from that fatally exposed direction and blanketed the *Canopus* with a perfectly placed patter of bombs. Tied up as she was, and unable to dodge, it seemed a miracle that only one of the closely bunched rain of missiles actually struck the ship, but that one bomb nearly ended our career then and there. It was an armor-piercing type which went through all the ship's decks, and exploded on top of the propeller shaft under the magazines, blowing them open, and starting fires which threatened to explode the ammunition.
>
> Four hours the devoted crew fought before all fires were finally out. When the magazines were examined, several crushed and exploded powder charges were found, mute evidence showing how close to complete destruction the ship and all on board had been. Nothing less than a miracle could have prevented a general magazine explosion at the time the bomb set off those powder charges, but miracles do happen. The engine of destruction had carried its own antidote, and it's fragments which severed pipes near the magazines had released floods of steam and water at the danger point, automatically keeping fire away from the rest of the powder. Our numbers just weren't quite up that day. {Sackett, p.12}

The ship is patched up and back in business on the very same day it's hit. A few days later, she's seaworthy again. I have many duties besides pumping oil, water, and different fluids off the ship. As time goes on, our supply gets low and in order to replenish it, we patrol Manila Bay during daylight hours all the way to Manila thirty miles away. There are five in the crew of a forty-foot motor launch equipped with empty 50 gallon barrels, a couple of pumps, and shallow water diving equipment. We have a 50-caliber machine gun mounted on the stern. Our Skipper, Commander Sackett, wants the gun mounted on the bow. He relents when we tell him we aren't going in to attack, but the gun is there so we can get out of any situation. We salvage quite a bit of oil from barges and small ships that were abandoned all over Manila Bay.

On one occasion, we salvage a sailboat, which is partly submerged. This is going to be our getaway, if we need it. Another time, we spot a sunken barge in about ten feet of water. It's still in tack and covered with canvas. Red Christenson, who is the Boat's Mate 1st class and all-around handyman, goes down and cuts through the canvas over the hatch. We lift the hatch off and find it's a barge filled with Scotch whiskey.

We salvage twenty-four cases that day. We figure that when we get back on the ship, we will be considered "millionaires" because whiskey and cigarettes are at a premium. Our Chief Warrant Officer, a hell-of-a nice guy, finds out about the whiskey we liberated from the barge. He liberates twenty out of twenty four cases for the officers. We end up with four cases of Scotch whiskey, which is still pretty good.

The next day we go out with better salvaging equipment. We anchor by the barge and suddenly artillery shells begin falling all around us. The shells land close enough for water to spray our faces. We get out of there fast. We don't know where the artillery is coming from. I find out the next day that it was the U.S. Army on Corregidor that was shelling us. Apparently, they were trying to chase us away, so they could salvage the whiskey themselves. We go out again on the third day and find guys from the Army on a tugboat anchored next to the barge. They have all kinds of divers and equipment. They are well-equipped to retrieve the rest of the booze from the barge.

We are not allowed to drink aboard, so we get together with the guy who makes the ice cream, the gedunkman {ice cream man}. This is the first time I get drunk on ice cream. On nights when all the shops aboard are humming, the officers have wild parties with nurses and army officers who can get away from the front lines. This goes on night after night.

Commander Sackett wrote a brief description of the officers' shipboard parties from his perspective;

> Nearly every evening, Army officers and nurses who were able to snatch a few hours leave from their duties, gathered on board the *Canopus*. We had refrigeration, excellent cooking facilities, and decent living quarters, which seemed heaven to them compared to the hardships in the field. To enjoy a real shower bath, cold drinking water, well-cooked meals served with real

butter, seemed almost too much for them to believe. When these favored ones returned to their primitive surroundings and described these "feasts" topped off with ice cream and chocolate sauce, they were often put in the same "dog house" as the optimists who claimed to have seen a fleet of transports steaming in. {Sackett, p.35}

As I mentioned before, my days are spent salvaging oil. One day, we get the chance to loot some of the stashed food the officers have hidden in their rooms, and we also take back some of our stolen Scotch whiskey. We take advantage of the opportunity when no one is aboard to go up to the officers' quarters and rummage around their rooms.

After the first deadly bombing attack in Mariveles Bay, Captain Sackett tells us to leave the ship and bivouac on the shore when the air raid alarms go off. The only men who stay aboard are four or five engineers, who remain down in the fire room to keep the boilers going. The Mariveles Bay area is pattern bombed by the Japanese almost every day.

The Japanese even bomb the Mariveles Section Base Hospital. The hospital is clearly marked with red and white crosses {according to the rules established by the Geneva Convention}, but Japanese bombers still burn the hospital to the ground by dropping incendiary explosives on it. The sign of the Red Cross had been formally established in the original Geneva Convention of 1864. In 1919, Japan officially joined the International Federation of Red Cross and Red Crescent Societies, which strictly prohibit the bombing of hospitals as a violation of international law. Apparently, their membership in the humanitarian organization was a complete sham.

Another time we are out all day picking up oil from various barges in Manila Bay from four in the morning to four o'clock in the afternoon. As usual, we come back aboard the ship and transfer the salvaged oil into the ship's tanks. We finish the job and decide to go ashore. Five of us are starting down the gangway, when an air raid alarm goes off. We run forty yards along the series of floats, which act as gangways from the ship to the land. We reach the land and keep running. When we look up, we see a dive-bomber coming straight at us. I glance up just as he releases his bombs. I see six bombs in the sky directly above me. I thought this was it! I figure he got us. We dive into the dirt. The bombs explode on the hill in front of us, covering us with dirt, rocks, and debris. We quickly dig ourselves out and we are up and running again {probably broke the record for the 100 yd dash}. When we get to safety, we find the Chief is missing. We run back and dig him out. He was buried up to his neck.

He said, "I thought you SOB's had left me to die."

Such things like that happened, of course, never recorded.

During another bombing attack, we take shelter on the beach under a washed-out section beneath a cliff. We take refuge in about two feet of space naturally carved out by the water. We lay there and wait for the bombing raid to get over. Suddenly, we hear a loud explosion and feel the ground trembling beneath us. We watch rocks, dirt, and other pieces of the cliff landing out in the bay. When it is all over, we go to the top of the cliff to check the damage. The bomb had struck the cliff directly above us. It blew a hole in the ground ten feet deep down to the granite above our heads.

Another time, I have the midnight watch with another guy at the head of the bay in a rice paddy. The Filipino Scouts have an AA battery of three-inch guns. In order to give them a rest, we sailors take guard at night. It's a dark night and you can't see very well, but I stare toward the jungle. After about four hours, I see someone crawling toward us. So, the two of us take aim and start firing as fast as we can; scary. We give no warning. The scouts get up and join us. Then, all is quiet. But, then something runs toward us from the dark. Six of us firing, and what do you think it is? A big dog! I guess we woke him up. None of us make a hit and he runs away.

A year later, I was telling this story to a group of POWs and an Army Captain came up to me after and said the dog we thought we shot at was actually him taking a short cut across the paddy, after spending a night in a cathouse. I never knew there was one within 50 miles. This is the way it was then. He said our shots were close and he sobered up fast.

Another time, the Japs land behind the main line on Bataan about five miles from our ship. A landing party is organized and we call it Bridget's Brigade. Frank Bridget is the Navy's Lt. Commander in charge. Their objective is to contain this attacking Japanese force until the Army can relieve them. I am not in this landing party, but on the tenth day, I am with the rescue party sent to carry out the wounded and the dead. Scary detail!

Commander Sackett explained the strategic rationale for the formation of Bridget's Brigade;

> Mariveles harbor seemed to be well defended against surprise attack by the Naval forces clustered around it and the Army had stabilized a front about twenty miles further north, on the other side of Mariveles mountain—but what about the seacoast between? Most of it was very rugged, and backed up by thick jungle, but the one road which provided the only line of communication to the front lines passed quite close to the sea at many points. Com-

mander Francis Bridget, who had been left in charge of the remnants of Naval aviation in the Philippines, did not think this tenuous life line was adequately defended by the Army against a sudden landing on the coast. {Sackett, p.22}

Commander Bridget has approximately one hundred and fifty Naval aviation men under his command, many of them ground crews who are out of work after their planes were destroyed by the initial Japanese bombing raids on the American airfields in the Philippines. He also recruits a hundred and thirty sailors from the *Canopus*, a handful of survivors from the Cavite Naval yard, eighty men from the Ammunition Depot, and about a hundred Marines.

Supplies are extremely limited for Bridget's Brigade. They have a difficult time finding rifles and ammunition for all the men. They run out of canteens, so they have to use tin cans. The Navy sailors dye their white uniforms a khaki color. The cooks make a strong batch of coffee and everyone soaks their whites in it. Most of the men have never been in combat. Many of them have only received limited field training. The Marines give the sailors and aviators a "crash course" in infantry warfare.

Commander Sackett described the Bridget Brigades' first contact with the enemy;

> Thus equipped, mostly with boundless enthusiasm and determination, the motley array sallied forth one day late in January for a preliminary hike to the coast to harden them up. At the base of Mt. Pucot near the sea, they met an agitated group of soldiers who had just been chased by the Japs from their signal station on the mountain top. Apparently, a landing had been made on nearby Longoskawayan point the night before, just as Bridget feared, and the invaders were working their way inland toward the vital communication road.

> Here was "field training" with a vengeance for our budding infantrymen. Figuratively thumbing their manuals, they hastily deployed in accordance with the best traditions of the book, and advanced in a line of skirmishers. Contact was established as might be expected, and the maneuver described as "The Assault" in the next chapter, drove in the advance patrols of the surprised Nipponese.

> The strength of the main forces next encountered convinced our boys that they had a "bear by the tail", and since the book failed to provide the proper procedure in such a contingency, they threw it away. Five days of what was

probably the weirdest jungle fighting in the history of warfare ensued, with all accepted principles violated, and no holds barred. Adjacent units were unable to maintain contact with each other during the night, so, of course, the Japs took advantage of this with their famous infiltration tactics. However, this did not have the intended results, because our boys, not having been indoctrinated into the ancient Army principle that it is fatal to be out-flanked, simply held their ground and sent back detachments to clear out the annoying intruders behind their lines. {Sackett, p.24}

Bridget's improvised Naval battalion is able to stop a vastly superior Japanese force from overrunning Mariveles behind the main lines of Fil-American forces. Veteran Filipino Scouts eventually relieve Bridget's Brigade and the improvised fighting force is sent over to Corregidor to augment the Fourth Marines' beach defenses.

Our ship, currently under the command of our Exec Lt. Commander Goodall, a great guy {a Prince}, reinforces two motor launches with metal plates and arms them with cannons and 50-caliber machine guns. We call these improvised attack boats "Mickey Mouse Battleships". Goodall's plan is to use the attack boats to strike caves the Japs are using to hide in on the shore at Longoskawayan point. They are successful the first day and bring back four wounded Japs and their arms. The prisoners are tied down to hospital stretchers and brought to Corregidor to get their wounds treated. Most of the prisoners close their eyes and won't look at us. Many Japanese soldiers do the "honorable" thing and kill themselves before they are captured. It is very rare that Japanese soldiers surrender. Most of them fight to the death.

The second day is a disaster. Jap dive-bombers sink one attack boat and badly damage the other. We have to bring the wounded back over land to the ship. There are five sailors wounded badly in the attack. Commander Goodall has his heel blown off, and that is the last I see of him until after the war is over. After the war, he was the commanding officer at Anacosta Naval Station in Washington. When I met up with him, he told me he'd get me transferred to his station and get me promoted to Chief Warrant Officer. I never took him up on the offer.

Another time, I am on lookout duty on a spire of rock thrust upward about 150 feet. It's an ideal place to watch for enemy planes. A rope ladder leads up to the top. The lookout is above Seaman's Cove, where the PT boats are stationed {hidden of course}. Seaman's Cove is a smaller bay near Mariveles Bay, which is mostly covered by overhanging trees. I am up there and I can see where the *Canopus* is anchored on one side and I can see PT boat sailors working on their boats on the other side. While looking down, I see two men come flying out of a PT boat and then hear an explosion. I watch them land in the water. They come back to the surface and swim back to the boat. I talk to them a few days later when they are alongside the *Canopus* for repairs. It seems one guy lit a cig {cigarette} and that's what caused the explosion in the engine room. The explosion blew them right up through the hatches.

Everyday there is something going on. Every night a Jap airplane glides over us and drops a bomb just to hone our nerves. Our records are kept in a tunnel {King's Hotel} about a mile from the ship. If we have any business there, we walk up there in the early morning. I am not warned about the Jap plane that likes to strafe the road on occasion. My morning is his occasion and we have to hit the dirt pronto! He is a good shot, but misses the both of us. The sailors name the tunnel "King's Hotel" and Commander King is proud of that sign, not realizing the King Hotel is the best whorehouse in Manila. Of course, that is news to me.

Another time, two barges pull alongside, which are loaded with butchered sides of meat from Corregidor. It seems their cold storage plant was bombed out. These sides of meat are from the mules that are being killed from the bombings. Our ship is the only place to store the mule meat. Our storage is big enough, but after a week we have to get rid of it because it is starting to smell!

The army sends trucks to pick up most of it for the front line troops. Everyday soldiers come aboard.

I talk to one guy and ask him, "How is the mule meat?"

"Fucking great." He responds, succinctly. "It's the best food we've had for months!"

He tells me their previous rations for the day were a can of salmon and a pound of rice for each squad, which consists of eight men. I don't know how they last as long as they do {five months}. I swap a carton of cigs for a Garand rifle. I am the only one on the *Canopus* who has one. This doesn't last.

Another time, Jap dive-bombers try to sink a small ship anchored in Mariveles Bay. The ship flies a Chinese flag. The planes dive-bomb the ship, but we can tell they will miss from the angle they are coming. We watch the bombs hit the water and skip over the ship. As the planes pull up after their bombing run, our ship and the ammunition depot, which is located on the other side of the bay, opens fire. We can't fire at them before this because we would be shooting at each other. I watch this go on for nearly two hours. Finally, we shoot one down. We send out a boat because the pilot bailed out, but we find nothing.

An hour later, a Jap biplane, looking for his downed buddy, comes close to where we are staying on the beach near a rock formation. He flies so close that I can see his face clearly. Everyone fires at him. I can see tracer bullets going right through the plane. I stop firing and give him a salute. He was a lucky SOB that day. Something is going on all the time. I don't have time to think about the situation. Some of us have been wounded by the enemy.

We have two meals per day, one before dawn and one after dark. When I see and talk to a soldier from the front, I consider myself lucky being in the U.S. Navy. I can now see the handwriting on the wall. We are doomed.

Before we lose all our P-40 fighter planes, I witness many dogfights. The zero is faster and more maneuverable. One time, I see one of our China gunboats save a P-40. He is diving between two of them, hoping to lure the zero into their crossfire, but the zero seems to stop and pull up. The P-40 escapes. Everyday the Japs bomb Corregidor, which we watch from where we are camped during the day.

Our AA guns on Corregidor hit a Jap formation flying at 28,000 feet and all of them are either shot down or break formation. Great shooting! I later found out that one of our subs brought in ammunition that could reach that high.

Every once in a while, ships would hit a mine. I never knew what side they were on. The infamous sub, "the *Squalus*" that sank in 1939 was renamed the *Sailfish* and we service her at least twice. We service subs until late February, 1942. A lot of our officers stow away on them and escape. It was rumored that our Chief Engineer stowed away on a sub. I should have done the same, as they were not punished. They said the sub got underway while they were visiting. Some story!

I found out that fifty-four officers stowed away on my old sub, the *U.S.S. Permit*. They just happened to be put on a work detail on the sub when they got underway. Have you ever heard of an officer being put on a work detail? Apparently, they had the inside information, which we weren't privy to. We were about to be massively over-run by the Japanese forces. The enlisted men were always kept in the dark about what was going on.

Many times, large groups of high-ranking officers are officially sent away from the battle zone on submarines. Navy sailor, Hank Henderson, describes one such instance in his diary:

> Jan. 2, 1942. All flag personnel were assembled on the *USS Canopus* for assignment to submarines that would ultimately take them to Australia. This included everyone except submarine spare parts personnel. When the submarine officers left the area, us so called stragglers were fair prey for any and all dirty details the Army could come up with. {Henderson, PT 1, p.2}

Early February, 1942, General MacArthur sends notices to all units that hundreds of planes and thousands of men are on their way. It's a morale builder, but I for one don't fall for it. I spoke to the sub sailors who saw what happened at Pearl Harbor and they said the whole fleet was sunk!

Also, in February, 1942, I make out a ten thousand dollar insurance policy, just in case I am pushing up daisies later on. I also extend my enlistment two more years. I was planning on going out of the service, but Tojo changed my mind just recently.

March, 1942. Boy, those dog-faces {Army soldiers} in the front lines are taking a beating all this time with hardly any relief. Every night the artillery duels go on for hours. The port side must be okay because the Japs aren't here yet.

Early April, 1942. Things are pretty much the same around here, but something big is happening. You know that before there's a big storm, there's always a lull. I settle into a daily routine and then the PT boats {four of them} leave our area and later we find out MacArthur had already escaped to Australia in early February {about the same time he issued the "help is on the way" bulletin}.

General Wainwright is promoted to the Lieutenant General in charge of all the remaining U.S. forces in the Philippines. General Wainwright is very popular with the Fil-American forces. By contrast, many of the troops vilify MacArthur and nickname him "Dugout Dug" for spending most of his time hiding in the Malinta tunnel on Corregidor {before running away to Australia}. Unlike "Dugout Doug", Wainwright spends a lot of time with the front line troops in the line of fire.

We have the sailboat ready to go, but the officers take it five days before Bataan falls and escape into the night. It seems they were given permission to do this. I guess they are more important than us sailors! When we originally found the sailing yacht, it was badly damaged and was not sailable. My friend, Red Christianson, worked for days to repair the yacht, make it sailable, and now it had been stolen by guys who had nothing to do with salvaging the craft.

My old submarine, the *U.S.S Permit*, was originally supposed to take MacArthur out of Corregidor. Apparently, he changed his mind and decided to escape on the PT boats instead. Four PT boats took MacArthur, the President of the Philippines, and all the high brass to safety. They were following one another, carrying extra fuel in barrels on board for the long trip.

The next morning, down around Mendora, the Ensign who was the Skipper of the 37-boat thought he saw a Japanese destroyer following them. They threw all the extra gasoline over the side, so they could lighten the load and get away. It turned out it was just another PT boat.

The PT boat was dead in the water. The submarine, *Permit*, came by later and picked up the stranded sailors. I spoke with guys who were on the crew of the abandoned PT boat, after the *Permit* picked them up and brought them to Corregidor. When they got to the island, a junior officer on the Permit, Lieutenant Flashenhauer, let it slip to the Army forces on Corregidor that they had the survivors of the PT boat on the *Permit* with them. The Skipper of the *Permit* was going to let them stay on the submarine and take them out with them. When Lt. Flashenhauer let it slip, the Skipper was ordered to kick them off the submarine. They were later captured on Corregidor and taken prisoner with the rest of us.

The Chief Petty Officer of the rescued crew of the PT boat said to me, "If I ever get back to the United States, I'm going to kill that son-of-a-bitch, Flashenhauer."

I met Flashenhauer years later after the war was over. Basically, we had two classifications of officers. They were either "a Prince" or "a prick". Flashenhauer was a prick.

An officer was a prick if he always went by the book. There was no flexibility with them. Good officers, "the Princes", would sometimes look the other way to help their men. Not so, the pricks.

In 1940 we were up at quarters one time and the Chief held us for an inspection. An inspection party came led by a Lieutenant Peterson. He looked like his head had gone through a meat grinder. One eye was shut and he was really banged up bad. It turned out that Lt. Peterson was looking for someone who beat him up. Apparently, somebody went up to his room, grabbed the curtain on the side of the door, and wrapped it around Peterson's head. Then, the guy beat the shit out of him while the curtain was around his head, so he couldn't see who was doing it. Peterson wanted to inspect all the sailors to see if any of us had bruised hands.

Whenever Peterson had the deck and everyone was lined up to go ashore, if he found any little thing out of the way, he would take your liberty card away and put it in the box so you couldn't go ashore. Years later, I was at a reunion in a bar in New York where I met this guy who we suspected had done the deed to Peterson. He was an old buddy of mine who we had nicknamed "Snake".

I said to him at the bar, "Snake, you must have been the one who beat Lt. Peterson up."

Snake said, "I don't know about that. All I know is the guy who did beat him up was wearing gloves."

Now I knew why Peterson couldn't find anyone with bruised knuckles at the inspection. Four days later, they transferred Lt. Peterson off the ship.

A week or two after that incident, three or four guys came aboard who were called "replacements". They were dressed like sailors, but we could tell they were really Naval Intelligence. We could tell they were officers because their hands were lily white as if they hadn't done a day's work in their lives. They stayed aboard for two weeks, trying to get some information about who beat up Peterson. If anyone knew who it was, they never said anything.

Snake stayed in the service and retired as a Chief Warrant Officer. Every time he had gone up on deck as a sailor, Peterson found something wrong with his uniform. The men of the Asiatic fleet didn't take any crap from anybody.

One by one, our officers disappear, so that when Bataan finally falls on April 8th, 1942, we only have our Skipper, two Lt. Commanders, a Lt. JG, and two Chief Warrant Officers left. Still, the parties go on every night, while we work our asses off. Can I say more? They are still drinking what we had salvaged earlier.

Our group, the "Oil Kings", is lucky because we use alcohol for test purposes. But the tests cease, so we can't let it go to waste. We still have the ice cream man freeze the booze into the ice cream. It's the best tasting ice cream I ever had.

Captain Sackett issues morale-building bulletins, describing inspirational feats achieved by American soldiers. One bulletin describes an Army Major who goes alone behind enemy lines and covertly kills Japanese soldiers. To prove how many Japanese soldiers he kills, he cuts off one of their ears and brings it back with him.

One night, we are issued 45 pistols and our Chief is showing us how to field strip them. While showing us the safety's, I pull the trigger and it goes off with a bang. It just barely misses the six of us in the small compartment. I dig a piece of the casing from my arm, but nothing is ever said about it.

7

Last Stand: Corregidor

April 7th, 1942. We get the word that Bataan is about to surrender. It's about midnight. We receive orders to scuttle the ship and take off for Corregidor. We can hear some of the big guns on Corregidor firing over our heads to delay the Japanese army's southward advance toward Mariveles Bay. It sounds like the world is coming to an end with all the explosions on Bataan. Everything of value in Bataan is being blown up and nearly all at once. Everyone gets into our motor launches, except the scuttling crew of ten men. They back the ship out into the channel and sink it by flooding the forward magazines and torpedo lockers, just like that.

We, in the small boats, are leaving Mariveles Bay when the Army blows up three tunnels on the side of the bay. One tunnel is full of gasoline. The whole mountain rains down on us. One boat is hit and we lose our Warrant Officer, a great guy. Some of the falling stones are as big as houses. Luck stays with me and we get out just as the Jap tanks are pulling into the docking area. Next stop Corregidor, the Gibraltar of the Far East, so they say.

We leave Bataan behind and land on the north side of the heavily-fortified island of Corregidor, which faces Bataan from a distance of two miles. Space is extremely limited on Corregidor. There are 9000 men on the island, including tons of supplies and ammunition. It turns out we are extremely lucky to escape to Corregidor. Originally, the commander of the16th Naval District, Captain Hoeffel told Captain Sackett that no American Navy forces were going to be evacuated to the fortified island. A short time later, General Wainwright agreed to accept a single Philippine Scout regiment and all the remaining Naval forces in the Mariveles area to help the Marines defend Corregidor's beaches.

If we had remained behind in Mariveles, we would have been captured and forced to participate in the infamous "Bataan Death March". Eleven-hundred Americans and ten thousand Filipinos were murdered by Japanese soldiers during the vicious 65-mile march from Mariveles to San Fernando. Those who survived the grueling death march to San Fernando were packed into sweltering steel box-cars to be transferred 25 miles to the infamous Prison Camp O'Donnell {where many more prisoners were killed by abuse and starvation}. Many helpless prisoners were killed for falling behind in the march and many others were killed for sadistic sport. There were reports of Japanese soldiers tossing Americans into the path of oncoming tank columns. If any of the starving or thirsty prisoners tried to get water by the side of the road, they were instantly bayoneted. Anyone who fell behind was beaten, shot, or stabbed with swords and bayonets. When sick prisoners fell by the side of the road from exhaustion, their buddies were forced to bury them alive. Filipino civilians who attempted to give the starving prisoners food or water were bayoneted by Japanese soldiers. As I said, we were extremely lucky to be accepted on Corregidor.

We thought we would have some kind of accommodations on the island, but they landed us on an upwardly-sloping area and we were told to dig in. We didn't go to the dock because the new powers in control figured that was where the Japs would shell. All day we watch the Japs bombing Bataan from the shores of Corregidor. They only bomb the Rock several times that day.

The digging is hard, for the soil is like concrete, so we take our time. About one hour after landing, the shells start falling among us. The deafening explosions throw off all sense of equilibrium. Splinters of rock and pieces of dirt fall onto our heads like black hail. The digging is sped up and my friend, Harold Lundberg, and I dig a hole big enough to get our heads in, leaving our asses exposed.

Every time a shell lands close, I say "And may God have mercy on our souls."

When there is a lull in the shelling, we stand up and Harold swings on me and says, "Don't ever say that again."

Two guys next to us dug a great foxhole. A shell lands between them and blows them out and they never got a scratch.

We stay there that night and the next morning we move to the south side of the island. We are two days without food and water. I am not used to this arrangement. We arrive at a heavily-fortified trench called Geary Trail, where we stay until the Japs invade the island on May 5th, 1942.

Geary Trail. It is a well-protected area located just below Battery Crockett, four 12" disappearing guns, and battery Geary, four 12" mortar cannons. Battery Geary can fire 360 degrees, while Crocket can only fire toward the sea at 180 degrees. These are only two of many heavy gun batteries placed in strategic defensive positions all over the fortified island. We are located about a mile from Malinta Hill. As I mentioned before, Corregidor is shaped like a giant pollywog, and Malinta Hill is located halfway down the tail. It rises up about three or four hundred feet. The headquarters for all the forces on Corregidor is located in a tunnel blasted straight through Malinta Hill.

The Jap Navy will send in a small craft, either a destroyer or minesweeper, just to test our guns. We watch several displays of accurate gunfire, but they stay just out of range.

We are now a part of the 4th Marine Regiment, a reserve battalion. At the time, I never realized exactly what a reserve battalion is. A reserve battalion is thrown into the battle wherever the fighting is the fiercest to help the troops being hit the hardest. Bayonet drills and practical infantry warfare are being pounded into us. We are willing pupils because we all know our lives are at stake. It's a strong feeling, this *I don't give a damn* feeling, when just a short while back all I could think about was going home. Sometimes, when I get a chance to think, I realize we're doomed. Help is never going to arrive soon enough to do us any good. If only we had something to fight back with! Every time I think of it, it makes my blood boil. We figure this will be a fight to the finish, like the Alamo in San Antonio, Texas.

My counterpart, Hank Henderson, had similar improvised battle training by the U.S. Marines:

> They {the Marines} were put in charge of training us in the use of the rifle, bayonet, pistol, hand grenades, knife, garrote, and hand to hand combat. Boy! They made Marines of us in short order. I got so adept with the Enfield rifle that during the invasion of Corregidor, when I got one of the enemy in my sights, he was a downed man. {Henderson, PT 1, p.2}

The Japs start shelling us and they never let up, even to cool their guns. The Japanese had amassed more than 400 heavy guns on the shores of Bataan, ranging from 75mm guns to 240mm howitzers. They launch a never-ending assault of explosive shells at us. Corregidor fires many outgoing rounds right over us. The rotating band comes off and they are worse than the shelling. We catch all the short rounds.

The constant noise of the exploding shells is horrific. A human being feels pain in the ear at 140 decibels. At 200 decibels, a person's body equilibrium is thrown off balance, neural activity is disrupted, and lungs can rupture. Just to give you an idea of what we are going through, the 240mm shells fired from Japanese howitzers explode at 200 decibels or higher. Speech is impossible, thought is disrupted, and we move as if we are in slow motion. It seems like an understatement to say we are being subjected to an almost non-stop acoustic assault.

April 24th, 1942. Battery Geary engages in an artillery duel with a Japanese howitzer firing from the shores of Bataan. The constant thundering is relentless. The howitzer also fires at Battery Crockett, which can't fire back because it's pointed away from Bataan toward the open sea. A massive barrier of earth-filled oil drums protects the rear of Battery Crockett. A four hundred pound shell blasts through the drums in a blinding burst of fire. Jagged pieces of shrapnel shoot from the explosion like airborne razor blades. Raging fires consume the lower passages of the battery. Some of Crockett's gunners are injured and killed. Surprisingly, only one of Battery Crockett's guns is knocked out.

Far above us on the mountain, Fort Drum fires back at the howitzer in retaliation. We figure it must have scored a hit on the howitzer because it finally falls silent. The silence doesn't last. A short time later, Battery Geary comes under fire from a smaller Japanese cannon. The thundering continues. Japanese aircraft roar overhead, dropping bombs. The sound of thunder intensifies as the ammunition dump between Battery Crockett and Hamilton is struck, igniting a massive fire.

On April 25th, 1942, the shelling is concentrated on the two batteries above us. Then, for two days and nights we are constantly bombarded with 240mm shells. I figure that if I'm lucky enough to survive, I'll be deaf by the time this is all over. The digging is in earnest now. Ten of us have dug a tunnel ten feet into the hillside ten feet apart and then connected. It's the only way to keep from getting killed. We still lose about twenty men at that time. Then, a mighty explosion blocks out all the light {from the sun}. We figure we've had it.

I am in the back of the tunnel and I have the digging tools. I pass them toward the entrance and lo and behold, we aren't buried. Just a lot of dust. We run to the head of the trail, where it makes a turn, where the wind blows the dust away. Wow! That was the biggest explosion on the island.

The Japs blow the top of the mountain off with 240mm shells, exposing Battery Geary's ammunition storage rooms. The ammunition explodes, causing a cataclysmic blast. They had finally knocked out both batteries. We send a rescue party up the hill to dig out the soldiers who are buried. They are buried deep. We have to move heavy pieces of blasted concrete to get them out. As soon as we get there, the Japs pepper the area with 105mm anti-personnel shells. Surprisingly, only five soldiers are killed during the rescue. This is a day I'll never forget if I live to be 100, which I intend to do. I later found out that some of our mortar cannons weighing five tons were found two miles away on the other side of the island. The exploding shells had been powerful enough to blow the five-ton guns clear across the island. Wow! Just like the fourth of Julys we used to have back in the USA.

April 27th, 1942. We receive word that B-25's have bombed Tokyo, Japan. Score one for the good guys! We are issued six hand grenades and taught how to use them. At that time, I realize I am not made for making war. I am made for making love. What a strange world. Our outfit is in the Fourth Battalion, Fourth Regiment, Marines held in reserve. All our squad leaders are Marines. A squad consists of eight men.

The Japs have us surrounded and they have a long-range cannon on the Caviti side of Manila Bay, about 12 miles from us. We call it the Caviti Express. They hit the island randomly. They have no set target. As I mentioned before, I have the only M-1 rifle and I fall in love with it. But, I didn't know how to field strip it. So, I ask a Chief Gunner's Mate to show me. We are kneeling just off the ditch in the road when suddenly he pushes me off the road. A shell comes careening out of the sky and explodes in the road with a deafening roar. My Garand rifle is blown to pieces. The bomb also blows apart our makeshift shower, which we rigged up by tapping a spring on the side of the road. I asked him how he knew a shell was heading our way. He had no explanation for it. He just said he had a feeling about it. Another close call. That was the last I saw of my M-1. I was issued a World War I rifle still packed in grease, a Marlin. Good gun, but slow firing compared to the M-1. Ammunition was the same; .306

May 3rd, 1942. The American submarine, *Spearfish*, slips through the Japanese blockade and minefield surrounding the island. It picks up the last twenty-five passengers to leave Corregidor. Thirteen of the passengers are women {twelve nurses and one officer's wife} and twelve are high-ranking officers. Our former Skipper, Commander Sackett, is finally able to escape, after staying with us for most of the siege. The *Spearfish* submerged two hundred feet under the sea and began its long journey through enemy lines toward Australia with its new passengers. There is no room left on the sub for fifty-four Army nurses and twenty-six Filipino nurses who are left behind.

At this time, I start smoking. It seems to calm my nerves. What a mistake. I take them because they are free. The shelling continues day and night. Then, we get our orders to move. Off we go marching with all the ammunition we are able to carry, including a few pineapples {hand grenades} apiece.

It takes us overnight to get to Malinta Tunnel, which is where all high-ranking officers are located. When we arrive in the tunnel, we are told to stand by for further orders. I am so tired, I just lay down and go to sleep. Later, I sit next to the headquarters tunnel, watching the officers eating and drinking coffee etc. Here we are hungry, thirsty, and tired, but no one offers us anything.

Hank Henderson gave his opinion of our situation in his diary:

> We had been subjected to seven days and nights of constant bombing, shelling and strafing without a letup of any kind. Food and water were in very short supply and had been for the past few months. The Japanese wasted their time invading us. If they had waited a few more days, we would have finished starving to death. This is the GOD'S Truth. In my opinion, this was one of the contributing factors of why so many of the POW's died so early after the surrender on Bataan and Corregidor. {Henderson, PT 1, p.3}

The Malinta tunnel runs straight through the hill. It's about 1000 yards long and has lateral tunnels branching off, containing hospitals and such. In order to get to the tunnel, we have to run toward it after a shell blows up at the entranceway. In other words, between shots. It is scary to say the least.

My squad leaves the tunnel about dawn the next day. We leave the same way we entered. Off we go running for about fifty yards. Then, lying flat, waiting for the next shell burst. We go to a fork in the road and find a Marine sitting behind some sandbags, bandaged around the head, staring straight ahead with a rifle still in his hands; dead. He has been shot between the eyes. That means snipers are already in back of us. Now I know it isn't just a nightmare. Two miles down the road, we get pinned down by machine gun fire. Two snipers are firing machine guns from a catwalk circling the upper level of a water tower. Someone crawls up and shoots them, so we can move forward.

Here I am and there is a war going on, and I have a rifle and some Japs have some rifles, but all the time I'm thinking I can't believe it is all just about knowing how to shoot a rifle. I now revert back to when I was a kid and play "follow the leader". But this is not good either, because them Japs have never heard of the game "follow the leader". All they know is how to "get the leader". At this rate, if it keeps up, I'll be the leader, so I figure maybe I should change my tactics.

The next thing I know, we are pinned down again. Luckily, we are in a depression in the road. The bullets are clipping the bushes in back of us, a few inches above our heads.

Our squad leader tells us, "Okay, men, let's get the bastard."

In unison, we all say, "After you Sarge."

We finally crawl around, spread out, and fire at anything that moves in front of us. Apparently, the Sarge thought better of being a hero.

We finally succeed in wiping out three machine gun positions and gaining a hill. There are more over the hill, so over we go again. We take chances a man would never normally take because we've read about these kinds of fellows, the

Japs, and know them like a book. I guess a fellow goes nuts. I see men falling all around me, but what can I do? I figure we're all going to get it eventually, so what's the difference?

Night comes and all is quiet. Still no food. What kind of outfit was this? Then, I figured it out. We weren't supposed to come back.

While I was fighting with my improvised Marine squad, Hank Henderson was defending the beaches. He described the beach invasion in his diary:

> May 5th, 1942. Wed. 22:30 hrs. The alert was sounded to repel boarders. The Japanese had landed and where? Right on top of us stragglers. Now I know this was not planned, but none the less, it happened that way. The battle raged until we were told the next morning to resist until noon, strip our guns, dispose of them, and surrender. However, by 10:00 hrs. this morning, we knew the end had come. After all, my Enfield was no match for the TANKS that had followed the infantry ashore and stomped us into the ground. As all of this was happening, a big shell dropped in on top of us. A small piece of shrapnel hit my left ankle and the concussion stunned me. {Henderson, PT 1, p.3}

The next morning, I use up fifty rounds firing at moving targets. I chicken out when I have a Jap all lined up about 150 yards away. He is unaware of us and rather than blowing his head off and alerting others to our presence, I let him go.

At about 10am, our Company Commander comes up and says, "It's all over. Get back to the Malinta tunnel and destroy your weapons. You're on your own."

Apparently, the U.S. forces are going to surrender at 11 AM. The Commander who gives us the news is an Army Air Force Lieutenant. We are quite a mixed up bunch.

The Anderson Sailors
Harry Earl Arthur Walter Roy

May 2005
Walter Anderson *brother*   Shawn Davis *great nephew* and *co author*
 Bill Davis *nephew*   Earl Anderson *protagonist* and *author*

May 2004
Earl and Walter Anderson at Veterans Memorial

WALTER-MEET AFTER 42 MOS JAP-P.O.W. - EARL

September 1945
Walter and Earl meet for the first time after Earl is liberated from a Japanese POW camp
where he was imprisoned for 42 months

The Anderson Family 1938
Top Row   Arthur Earl Ralph
Second Row   Roy Chester Harry Henry Carl Walter
First Row   Hazel Edith Hannah Evelyn Mildred

May 2004
Walter and Earl hold a picture of themselves when they first met in September 1945 after Earl was liberated

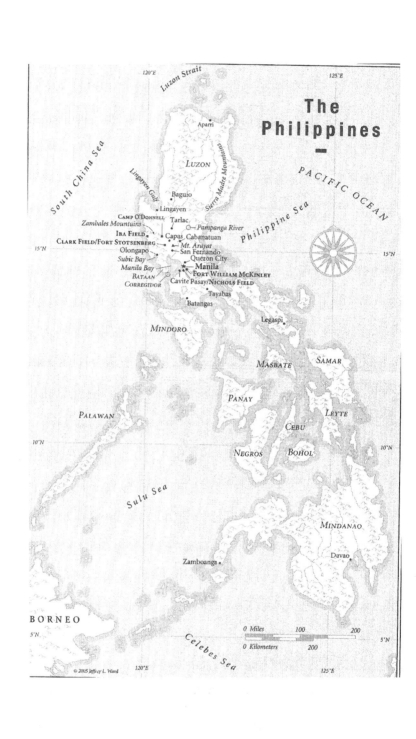

8

Surrender

Three other sailors and myself improvise a stretcher and carry a wounded man back to the Malinta tunnel. Getting back takes us about three hours. The Japs are still shelling the entrance to the tunnel. We get inside and collapse into a dead heap. Still no food or water. I scoop some water out of a drainage ditch and drink it. It tastes disgusting. Everyone is busting up rifles and equipment. The Japs are still shelling. Maybe they aren't going to let us pack in our chips?

It looks they are going to let us pack in our chips, because the Japs finally came into the tunnel. They weren't here for half an hour when a private hit me in the guts with a rifle butt. They order us out the opposite entrance. This story is getting to me so I'll stop for awhile. It's like a moving picture in my mind. Damn, I was hungry and thirsty.

My fellow Navy sailor, Hank Henderson, also had his first introduction to one of our Japanese captors:

> I don't know how long I was in this stupor. Some time later, I came to. My rifle had been fired for so long and so many times, that the protective wood around the barrel showed signs of being charred by the heat of this rapid firing. A Japanese soldier was nudging me with his bayonet and pointing in the direction of the 92nd Field Artillery garage. I didn't think I could, but he convinced me otherwise. We were all moved to this location to await further developments. {Henderson, PT 1, p.3}

All of us are outside and forced to lie down. Evidently, somebody didn't get the word, because there is still shelling and bombing going on up topside and on Ft. Hughes. We all sleep on the road that night.

Third day. I fill two canteens full of water. Now, I, too, have some water. Four of us stuck together and would stay together while on Corregidor. There is no sign that we are going to receive food. So, I suggest we go look for some. There are no guards around at the moment, so we take off. We wander up Malinta Hill and stop near the top, where we locate four well-equipped beds. They have nets and canvas to protect them from rain. It turns out to be Col. Howard's command post of the Fourth Marines.

All the luxuries of home. We can't find any food, but we locate lots of Scotch whiskey. I immediately fill both canteens with Scotch. No food, so we all get drunk and fall asleep on the beds that are very comfortable. This spot is well-located. From this location, the Marines could see all over the former combat zone. Also, there was a vent that went down to the Malinta tunnel in case of shelling. How nice.

The next thing I know, I am awakened by a bayonet being stuck in my chest, enough to penetrate my skin. He and six other Jap soldiers {North Koreans-they were as big as we were-some even bigger} wanted to know where the whiskey was. Japan had taken over Korea in 1906, so most of the Japanese Marines were North Koreans. We all scrambled around and found enough whiskey to satisfy them. They forced us to get up and strip off our clothes. This being done, they searched the clothes. The only thing of value they could find was our canteen bottles. We finally talk them into letting us keep them. If they had only known what was really in them, I don't know what they would have done to us. We had them both filled with whiskey. When they finished searching everything in the camp, they threw our clothing at us and told us to go down with the rest of the Americans. That was the last time I separated from the main body of Americans. That night could have ended much differently, if they had been in a difficult mood. Evidently, they were just out looting.

We go back down into the valley where we came from. We call this area "death valley" because everything has been reduced to rubble from the bombing and shelling. In peacetime, this area was a Filipino village. Now, it is only rubble.

Two days later, we are herded, 300 at a time, to the ill-famed 92nd garage area about two miles from where we were. Over eight thousand of us had been squeezed into a small area. I forgot about my canteens until we arrived at the 92nd garage area. Along the way, I picked up the tins of coffee that came with C-rations and stuffed them in a sock.

We don't eat any food for eighteen days. The five of us in our group live on Scotch whiskey and coffee. We would build a small fire and melt the soluble coffee from our C-rations into some water. A Scotsman once told me that whiskey was the staff of life. I believe him. We had one faucet of water and there were 8000 of us. One man in our group had to be in line twenty-four hours a day to get a gallon of water. The whiskey kept us going.

We sheltered ourselves with scrap metal and whatever else we could find. Everyone did the same. What a mad scramble. We built a little shack out of tin, canvas, and dirt to protect us from the sun and heat. It didn't take us long to figure out that they didn't want to feed us. Apparently, "get along as best you can" was their attitude, so we go out searching and finally pick up a little can chow. We get most of our food out of old gun positions that have been covered over. I learn quite a bit about cooking in this period. Of course, it does not taste like anything.

The only way you can get food from the Japs is if you go on a work detail. On the fourteenth day, I go on a detail, loading Jap ships with all the good food they had captured from us. The first thing I find is a can of anchovies with a key. I used to hate anchovies, but this time it is the best food I ever ate in my life. I am able to drink a can of condensed milk after puncturing a hole in the top. I stuff my shirt full of canned goods, as much as I can carry back to the 92nd garage. When I empty the food, we think the world is a better place. The food that I ate gave me diarrhea so bad, it was two days before I could eat again.

May 21st or 22nd, 1942. We are moved by ship to Manila. We are loaded on three transports and every inch of deck and below space is loaded with people. There are no toilets and 50% of the men had come down with dysentery. It was a nightmare. This was nothing compared to what was to come in the next three years of prison life. I got shook down and had to give up the 16 pesos I had hidden in my shoe. We arrive in Manila two days later, where we are loaded onto landing boats. They bring us as close to the beach as possible. Here, we have to jump out and swim ashore. Many people have to swim because they are dropped off in water that is pretty deep. I am able to wade ashore.

Hank Henderson had a similar experience a few days later:

> May 24, 1942. We were moved to some Japanese transports to carry us to Manila and into Bilibid Prison. I had a new blanket slung around my shoulder. A Japanese soldier on the small craft ferrying us to the transports swapped my new blanket for one that was full of holes. I thought this was a real good deal. HE WAS VERY convincing.

> May 25, 1942. The transports got underway. Instead of tying up to the docks in the port area, they went way out on Dewey Blvd. and dumped us off into the water. Now these were conventional landing craft and they could have went right onto the beach, but this was more fun. OLE Lucky me, I was Number One man in the front rank, right behind some cavalry horses.

> This was also a lot of fun. We made the Victory March from this point into
> Bilibid Prison. {Henderson, PT 1, p.4}

As soon as we hit the beach, we are lined up and marched off. This hike is through the heart of Manila, about an eight-mile course. This is a humiliation march; the Japs want to show the Filipinos they have conquered us. The guards keep us hopping. If a man was tired and fell by the road, he was beaten up. If he still did not get back up, he was left behind and eventually picked up later by a truck. About halfway, we stop and the Filipinos are allowed to give us water. They also give us cigarettes, candy, medicine, and ice cream on the side. Their actions re-affirm our faith in them.

Not surprisingly, the Filipino people hated the invading Japanese soldiers as much as we did. Even the primitive tribes of Filipinos living in the jungle hated the Japanese. I knew about one tribe, the Igorots, who were located just north of Subic Bay. The Igorots were medium-sized people who lived in the jungle and they were very friendly with the Americans during World War II. The Igorots killed any Japanese soldiers who wandered into their jungle territory. The Igorots had no problem surviving the Japanese invasion. The Japanese had learned to stay away from them. The Igorots would silently kill the Japanese soldiers and then disappear into the jungle. They didn't have any guns. They used machetes, blow-guns, and bow-and-arrows on the Japanese soldiers.

During peacetime, some Igorots visited our base. They brought a twenty-five foot python with them. They had the python strapped to a pole. The python gave off a strange, sweet-smelling odor. They carried it into the base and tried to sell it. Years before, the explorer, Frank Buck, came back with the largest snake ever captured in the world at that time. He supposedly captured the snake himself, but it was really the Igorots who captured it for him.

The Igorots helped train the Americans in jungle survival. Most survival training for the Army Air Corps was done in their area. The Americans figured if they could survive in the jungle without the Igorots tracking them down quickly, then they were successful in their course. Of course, the Igorots always found them eventually.

Later that day, we arrive at Bilibid Prison, an old Spanish prison. The next day, we are fed our first meal of steamed rice, some soup, and yes, some hot water. Of course, some of the men have canned food, but they are not sharing. It is dog-eat-dog from here on out. It's strange how men change under situations like this, but it happens. It didn't happen to everybody, but it did happen to the majority of men. As for myself, I don't have anything in the line of extra food or money, so I have to take what is given to me by the Japs. By this time I am down to 128 pounds soaking wet. My normal weight was about 160.

We stay in Bilibid four days and are moved out in a group of 500. On the night of May 27th, we are marched to the railway station, where we are loaded 100 men to a boxcar. The boxcars in the Philippines are about half the size of a U.S. boxcar. The trip to Camp Cabanatuan lasts all night. We are transported north for a total of about 60 miles. We have to stand up, we are packed in so tight.

Apparently, Hank Henderson was in a similar group of POWs being transported to Camp Cabanatuan by train. He wrote about the event in his diary:

> May 27, 1942. We were marched to the railroad tracks, to be hauled to Cabanatuan to the POW Camps. These box cars were the narrow gauge type, groups of one hundred men each were crowded into them to await transportation to our new home. There was no ventilation and several of us were almost overcome by heat exhaustion. We unloaded and stayed in a very crowded enclosure for the night. {Henderson, PT 1, p.4}

After the train ride, the Japs herd us into a schoolyard with a fence around it. That night, we sleep on the ground in the pouring rain. I tell my brother, Walter, what happens there the next morning. Two soldiers are beheaded because they don't move fast enough. We are marched about twenty miles to Camp Cabanatuan. I now know I'll be lucky to make it to my 23rd birthday.

9

Camp Cabanatuan

When we arrive at Camp Cabanatuan, I am walking on air. I guess I just barely made it. The Japs have four soldiers tied up to stakes at the entrance for us to see. They have been there a long time; they are in terrible condition. Two days later, they are executed by a firing squad for all to see. Graves are dug and they are forced to stand in front of them, and shot. Their crime was escaping and being captured. The date was around May 30th, 1942. I now weigh less than one hundred pounds.

Hank Henderson was also at Cabanatuan when the re-captured POWs were executed. He described the same situation in his diary:

> After we arrived at the camp, four men walked out the front gate and as they walked down the middle of the road, they were apprehended and brought back to camp. They were tied to some corner posts for the next two days without food or water.

> May 30, 1942. We witnessed our first execution of these four men. During the next two months, many, many of the POWs would die of disease. {Henderson, PT 1, p.4}

We find out later that some traitorous Filipinos had turned in the four escaped American POWs for a reward. The Japanese were offering rewards to anyone who turned in escaped prisoners.

The Japanese divide us up into groups of ten, which they call "scads".

They tell us if any one of the ten men in the group escape, the other nine men will be executed. We have a Marine in our group whose face is severely battered. He has open wounds on one side of his face. His last name is Wolf. He keeps saying, "I'm going under the wire tonight." We keep a watch on him all night. We figure if he takes off, we are all going to take off.

It is possible to get out of the camp. The only problem is you have to travel fifty or sixty miles through enemy territory until you reach the mountains. Some of the Filipinos are loyal and some are not. If we are turned in and caught, we know what to expect.

June-September, 1942. Here is my home for the next three and a half months. Camp Cabanatuan had been built for the Philippine Army just before the war started. Cabanatuan was now the holding camp for all U.S. POWs. From here, work details are sent out all over the Philippines. Some of the stories that come back are horror tales. Some people who come back are at death's door.

Hank Henderson was one of the POWs who were shipped out early on a Philippines work detail. He describes the experience in his diary:

> July 28, 1942. Three hundred of us were assembled with orders to go back to Bilibid in Manila to be further assigned to construct Air Bases.
>
> July 29, 1942. We marched down to the docks and boarded Japanese transports to be moved to Puerto Princessa, Palawan in the Philippine Islands.
>
> August 1, 1942. The ship docked at our destination and we were billeted in a deserted Philippine Army Scout barracks. From our physical immobility during the stay in Cabanatuan, we were so weak, it was almost impossible to work. We were immediately introduced to the VITAMIN STICK, now one of those was adequate incentive to work. As a result of this hard labor, our hands were bloody pulps from using the juji {pick axe} and the impi {shovel}. We worked almost naked in the boiling hot sun for the next twenty seven months. We constructed a 1200 meter landing strip with turn tables at each end. The jungle had to be cleared. Try cutting down coconut, mahogany, and bamboo clusters with primitive hand tools. Making cuts and fills with the juji and impi. Moving the soil in hand operated pushcarts on small light narrow rails. {Henderson, PT 1, p.5}

My friends and I are lucky not to get shipped out on any long-term Philippines work details. The Philippines work details are reputed to be very brutal.

During our time at Cabanatuan, we are completely unaware of the progress of the war. We are too worried about survival to focus on obtaining any information about how the fighting is going. Unbeknownst to us, the Japanese now control most of the Pacific. The Japanese are preparing to attack Australia by building an airbase on the island of Guadalcanal. The only good news is the American victory at the battle of Midway on June 4th-7th, 1942.

When World War II broke out, the United States had seven aircraft carriers compared to Japan's seventeen aircraft carriers. During the battle of Midway from June 4th-7th, 1942, the United States sank four Japanese aircraft carriers.

After all of the carnage and destruction involved in sinking the first three carriers, the Navy was ready to call off the attack and let the fourth carrier go. Admiral Nimitz stepped in and told them to go after the fourth carrier. The U.S. forces pursued and sank the fourth carrier, which destroyed Japan's capacity to directly attack the United States.

The battle of Midway in June, 1942 was the turning point of the war. The Japanese lost four aircraft carriers compared to the U.S. losing one carrier. The destruction of the four Japanese aircraft carriers at the battle of Midway caused the Japanese to turn away from Hawaii as a target and focus on the Dutch East Indies instead. This gave the U.S. a chance to recuperate and build up our Navy. With aircraft carriers, the Japanese could have supported a landing on Hawaii or the West Coast of the United States. At that early time in the war, we effectively had only about 200,000 men in the U.S. Army. By June, 1942, we had 500,000, which grew rapidly to 1,000,000. Also, at that time, the U.S. had no defenses against a Japanese landing on Hawaii or the West Coast. The battle of Midway woke the country up and got everybody behind the war one hundred percent.

However, the Japanese still controlled most of the Pacific. Australia was the only free country left in the South Pacific. In July, 1942, the Japanese began constructing an airstrip on the island of Guadalcanal, which is on the southern tip of the Solomon islands chain, to the northeast of Australia. From there, they were in range to attack Australia. The U.S Marines began their heroic campaign to take back Guadalcanal on August 7th, 1942.

Despite the momentous events in the outside world, things go on as usual for us. Poker and dice games are in progress all over the camp. Before the Rock fell, some men in the tunnels had access to money that was going to be destroyed, or apparently taken if the men wanted to. Well, some of these games are really big-time; thousands of dollars in every pot. Boy, what a fool's paradise this place is for some.

Some unscrupulous POWs take advantage of other vulnerable POWs. POWs, who are addicted to nicotine, are sometimes convinced to give up what little food they have for cigarettes. The result is they get plenty of nicotine, but they starve to death.

American truck drivers go daily from Cabanatuan to Manila for supplies with a Japanese guard. By bribing the guards, they are able to buy medicine at pharmacies there. Most are mercenaries and do it to make money off American POWs who are sick and dying. We do not have to work at camp except to maintain ourselves. Dysentery is the big killer and in our weakened condition, it kills many.

The Japs allow us to bury our dead once a week on Wednesdays. Why? I'll never know. The bodies are badly decomposed. We receive no medical attention, except from within, from each other. All kinds of old remedies show up. Some of them work very well. One of the old remedies is eating charcoal. Eating charcoal can cure most stomach ailments.

Pop Lundberg, myself, and another sailor team up. It's an even split on everything we have. Pop and I work together swell, but this other guy is a dope. Maybe he can't help himself like many men who have gone off their nut, so we gradually ease away from him and are on our own. Pop and I.

All the month of June we make out okay. I supply wood for the galley, where I am allowed to eat extra food and take all I can lay my hands on. Funny, that I never stole a thing in my life before. Now, it's dog-eat-dog and to hell with you. Yes, that's easy to say, but when someone you know is down and out, you forget this rule of prison life.

My closest shipmate, Pop, comes down with dysentery and almost gives up the fight. I volunteer and work for a Jap guard, making wooden go-aheads {shoes}. I receive a can of evaporated milk and a biscuit. I force Harold {Pop} Lundberg to eat the biscuit. Sometimes I have to chew it first because he is so dehydrated. It works and he survives.

10

Destination: Japan

There are so many deaths at camp, I decide to go on a work detail. The Japs want 300 Navy men to go on a detail. Harold Lundberg, Floyd Woodward, and I volunteer. We are shipped back to Bilibid Prison in Manila about September 13th, 1942. There are all kinds of civilian internees there with us in the prison. Some of them are newspaper correspondents. Some of them come up to us and say, "You know where you're going, don't you?" We say, "No, we have no idea." They say, "They're going to ship you to Japan. You're going to be the first group to go." Actually, it turns out we were lucky to get out of there then. Near the end of the war, the Japanese tried to ship thousands of POWs to Japan, as the American forces were advancing on them. Most of the POWs died when American planes and submarines sank the ships they were being transported on.

We stay in Manila about four days and board a Maru. All Japanese ships were called Marus. Maru means circle in Japanese. When Japan built their first modern ships, they made full circles after they were launched. We are going to Japan. I am glad about this because the work details in the Philippines are very bad. The newspaper correspondents had been right. We are the first group to be shipped to Japan. At the dock, we find out we are going to have some distinguished passengers. Twenty-seven high-ranking Army officers are with us. You would think that the Japs would show some consideration to these officers, but no. Down into the same hold they go. We are all locked into one hold below deck. There are over four hundred men placed in an area that we wouldn't squeeze that many animals into.

For the next ten days, we live in agony, taking turns to sit or sleep, faking dizzy spells so we can go topside for a breath of fresh air. Finally, the ship comes to a stop and we are herded down to a dock.

It takes us six days to get to Formosa {modern Taiwan}. The officers are marched one way and we are marched another way. We are lined up and deloused. After being in a dirty, stinking hold of a ship, they spray us with a solution that smells of rat dung. Our baggage, if you can call it that, is inspected for arms. Several weeks later, I saw some of the arms they missed. Colt forty-five revolvers, knives of all sizes and descriptions, and last but not least, enough hand grenades to blow up a battleship. They were all concealed in our baggage and kept in the hope that some day we may use them on these little brown brothers of ours. At this time of the war, the Japs were riding high. I guess they thought they were going to win, but I never believed it and never gave up.

We take a train ride lasting one day and one night, no food or water. It is a ten-mile hike to the POW camp. First, we are examined and our shoes are taken away from us. Evidently, they figure that we might escape if we're wearing shoes. But I say, "Where could we possibly go from here?" Next, we are forced to sign a paper, stating we will not escape and we are now guests of the Emperor. Naturally, we all sign, but I know that if I get the chance, I'll pull up stakes and haul. We are given a speech that lasts two hours by a Jap who looks like Boris Karloff, which is what we name him. All of the red tape takes us well into the afternoon. Before being dismissed, we are warned not to drink the water unless it is boiled.

This was easier said than done. Have you ever gone without water for days in the tropics? When they turned us loose, we all headed to the washstand where I drank gallons of delicious drainage water. By the time we finished washing our bodies and clothes, all we had left to do was dry our skin. Yes, but boy, what a relief.

This was supposed to be a model camp. It consisted of two long huts, mats on raised platforms with mosquito nets. At the end of the huts {nipa}, was a water tank. The main water supply came out of a bamboo pipe to a tee and these tees were wooden plugs that released the water. The water came out of the rice paddies that surrounded us. Surprisingly, no one got sick that I know of from drinking the water.

The next day is a workday. We make a two-mile hike to a riverbed full of rocks. Our jobs are to carry these rocks to the road and load them onto trucks. This is what we do for the rest of the stay from September 18th to November 19th, 1942.

September-November, 1942.
04:30 Tinko time-roll-call or "muster" for us
05:00-05:30 Tiser-physical culture or just plain torture
05:30-05:45 Mesi-Chow down on food, consisting of a bowl of 50% unpolished rice, 30% barley {moldy}. The second course is a small bowl of pipe-steamed tripe. The third course is a cup of green tea.

06:00 Work Parade-Here we are given a pair of canvas shoes, a pick, a shovel, or a yo-yo pole with two baskets.

While eating, we are instructed to sit cross-legged, Japanese-fashion, and to use chopsticks, which they furnish. We comply with these rules if a guard is watching, but when he isn't, we use a spoon or a fork and dream about steak and all the good food we ate before this all came about.

We are given Jap-English books to learn the Jap language, which we are supposedly going to use when the Japs take over the USA. They want to teach the U.S. how to be Japanese. We go along with it, as they are easy on us. They tell us that when they take over the United States, they are going to send us back and put us in charge of cities and towns. We pretend we are all for it. We say, "Wow, a whole city? Really?" We read their books and listen to their lectures. Of course, we know all this is never going to happen.

Eventually, they stop teaching us. Maybe they thought we were learning too fast. They are getting wise to the fact that we are just going along with it, and really don't believe anything they are telling us.

After two weeks, we are ordered out on the parade ground. Here, we stay for eight days and are questioned one at a time. They know all about me, my date of enlistment and qualifications. The amazing part about it is that they know my entire life history. Here I am, a little old sailor, and they knew all about me! They knew when I was born, when I enlisted in the Navy, when I went to boot camp, and what schools I attended. We found out later that they knew a Jap Code-breaker, Radio, was among us. They never did find him. Our treatment changes and the Japanese culture books are taken away.

How did the Japanese obtain all the detailed information about me? The answer is a mystery. They probably obtained the information from the records at our headquarters at Corregidor.

After the war, we found out who the mysterious Radio Code-man was. It was no surprise he could read, write, and speak Japanese. He was an expert Radio Tech and eventually built a short wave radio at our future camp in Yokohama, so we knew how the war was going. This info was given to us much later than when it happened. He took a dead man's ID to avoid detection.

We depart Formosa about November 19th, 1942. We are loaded on a Maru and arrive in Simonsinko in southern Japan. We take a ferry ride to Moji, which is the southern tip of Honshu Island. We are surprised at the good treatment. Japanese women feed us at train stops, mostly rice balls and dried fish. My spirits pick up.

11

Yokohama

Yokohama, Japan, November 28th, 1942. Pop and I arrive at the prison camp and we are put in a warehouse on the waterfront close to the fish piers. This was to prove to be our home for more than 2 ½ years. Pop weighs 106 pounds and I am 115 pounds. They have an industrial scale in the warehouse, which we use to weigh ourselves. We are allotted an insufficient amount of bed space, but that doesn't matter because we sleep next to each other for warmth.

The building in Yokohama is an old warehouse fitted with double bunks, Jap-fashion. Over 500 men crawl into a space that we wouldn't put 500 pigs in. There is no heating system, holes in the walls, blown-out windows, stinking toilets. Everybody is in a weakened condition with dysentery, malaria, and God knows what. I make it about twenty five times a day myself and Pop is much worse off. This is the lowest my spirits have been and I don't expect to ever leave here alive.

No sooner do we settle in, when a series of nine explosions shake us up. The warehouse building walls shake every time an explosion goes off. It seems there are nine French ships in Tokyo Bay. The French crews refused to give the ships over to the Japanese. They blew the ships up instead. The ships' crews are free French, not Vichy {the Vichy French collaborated with the Germans}. At that time, there were no sub or air attacks yet.

Our first day is rest and organization day. We are told that we will be working in a shipyard owned by Mitsubishi. At this time, Mitsubishi is Japan. The same is true in 2007. Mitsubishi pretty much controls what happens, at least where I am assigned. Mitsubishi owns extensive mines, aircraft factories, tank factories, and all kinds of heavy industry. They build all the Japanese Zero fighter crafts and twin-engine bombers. The military complex in Japan, similar to our own country, controls the country. They tell the politicians what to do and get all the money they want.

You can see the same thing happening everyday in this country. I believe the only way to counteract the corrupt political/military industrial alliance in this country is to reinstate the draft. We should not have an all-volunteer army. That way everyone has to serve-including the children of the politicians and military industrialists. They would all have kids who are in the service, so they might think twice about sending them to war. An all-volunteer army is not right for the country because the only people who are going to serve are the poor people. This is the way it has always been throughout history. One of the reasons I went into the service was because there was no work around. The bottom line was that I was poor when I volunteered.

At our camp in Yokohama, our guards are Japanese army and Mitsubishi workers assigned as guards. The civilian guards sometimes carry rifles without any ammunition. I guess they figured, where the hell could we escape to? White men in Japan would stick out like sore thumbs. Plans were made to capture a fishing boat and sail away, but it never amounted to much. At the last camp I was in, the guards all became civilian workers, except for a Jap commander and a Jap army sergeant. Most of the time, we didn't have any contact with them.

Yokohama 2nd day. We are issued work clothes and brought to the shipyard. The yard is about three miles from our quarters. I tell them I am a plumber, so I am assigned to the pipe shop. This is where they bend pipe for new ships under construction. I know that Japan can never win with their ancient methods of construction, and we POWs do nothing to help. We intentionally hold them back. We do as little as possible.

Our daily routine starts with "tinko time" or roll call every morning at 05:30. We assemble on the parade ground and the Japanese account for each of us. At 06:00 we have breakfast, which consists of a bowl of rice. At 06:30 we walk two and a half miles through central Yokohama to the shipyard. At 07:00 we start work.

The electric welder {Japanese} in the pipe shop is a pretty decent sort. He gives me rest periods and cigarettes. He asks the regular run-of-the-mill questions and treats me like a worker instead of a prisoner.

I work for two days and then have to stay in sick. What exactly is wrong I don't know, but I figure if I want to live, I have to snap out of it and get back to work.

My next job is located just outside the main shop where the flanges are cut out and straightened for fitting to the ends of pipe. My job is to chip and stack these flanges. They are red-hot. The furnaces are fed by coke and I have to keep them supplied.

This gives me the opportunity to leave the area and go to a pier where the coke is stored. I push a cart that carries about ten bushels of coke. This routine goes on and on, day after day. My strength returns somewhat, but the main cry is food. We never get enough to eat. Next to the shop is a Jap Navy galley. Every meal they throw away is better food than we get at camp. Some of the boys are going into these boxes and getting meat, fish, and rice. They say it's okay, but my pride holds me back, as my belly says go ahead. If I want to live, I will probably have to do the same.

December 4th, 1942. Today, one of my buddies brought me a mess kit of hot rice, which I ate. He later told me it came out of the swill box at the galley. That converted me. I threw pride to the four winds. If we were caught by the foo {guard}, we would sometimes get punched and slapped. But, this never stopped us from going after the extra food. Sometimes, a Japanese sailor would give us food right out of the galley. We carry sampan bags {garbage bags} with us as the opportunity arises.

At this time, the Marines at Guadalcanal were on their way to achieving victory after four straight months of heavy fighting. 23,000 Japanese troops were killed during the four-month-plus battle. Another 13,000 troops were evacuated. Unbeknownst to us, Japan had suffered its first major land defeat in the war.

My shop is eventually moved to a building located 18 feet away from the Jap Navy galley. I think I am in heaven. Day after day the cooks come over to my fire to get warm and naturally converse with me, some in English and some in Japanese—a few key words I know. They are all right, in that they give me food where and when I request it. Gradually, I get back in shape, and the winter months gradually wear off.

Days and weeks on end the routine is eat, work, sleep, and so forth, without one minute to yourself. One of the biggest hardships is the lack of soap to work with. The most disheartening thing isn't when the Japs say they will win the war. It is the number of deaths in the camp. Every day I come into camp exhausted and after eating my bowl of rice every night, attention is called and another mother's son is carried away. Twenty-nine Americans and fourteen others pass away this horrible winter.

May, 1943. Spring finally arrives and a man is able to take a few clothes off his bones and get clean again. But the work continues, ten hours a day, with only two days off a month. I nearly blow my fuse in early May with those pesty mosquitoes. They are a plague to us for the rest of the year.

As I mentioned before, most of our guards are civilian workers. While we are working at the shipyard, we see very little of them. We work alongside Japanese workers everyday. They are like any other worker in America. Many of them know very little about geography.

One time, a Japanese co-worker comes up to me and says, "We're fighting the Americans in Florida." I am shocked by the news, exclaiming, "You've got to be kidding!"

It turns out there's a group of islands around Guadalcanal and one of them is named Florida. We rarely get up-to-date information. We usually receive news that is about a month or two old.

The Japs have thousands of Korean school kids working at this yard and they hate the Japs probably more than us. They are paid mostly in cigarettes, which are used as a medium of exchange. The Koreans are always trying to exchange cigs for whatever we have to trade. I get along very well and carry on many trades with them.

Every night our quarters are like a Chinese bazaar. Men are walking around everywhere, swapping this and that. Cigs are used as a medium of exchange. I pick up trade items at camp, take them to the shipyard, and trade them for cigs. There are payoffs to guards, workers, and fellow POW's. My share is over 50% and I have nothing invested except the risk of being caught. It is exciting, so it keeps me going.

There is a Japanese guard at our camp, who we nickname "Charlie Chaplin" because he walks like his namesake. We get along well with him because he is always looking for a payoff. The guards periodically inspect us for contraband. They conduct strip searches, where we take all our clothes off and they go through our clothing to see what we have. Charlie walks up to me, kicks my clothes, and says, "Tobacco?"

I would say, "Yea." Then, he would walk away without inspecting my clothes. Later, he came by for his payoff. I would give him some of the cigarettes I got from trading with the Korean kids at work.

One time, I arrange a major trade with the Korean kids in the shipyard. One of our guys had been sent a beautiful pair of dress shoes from home. I don't know how the package got through, but somehow it did. Since we obviously have no need for dress shoes in our camp, he wants me to trade them for him and get him a good deal. I bring one of the shoes into the shipyard and show it to the Koreans. I make a deal with a Korean kid and tell him I'll bring the other shoe the next day. The next day, I give him the shoes and he gives me 3800 cigarettes for them. It is a pretty large bundle, so I have to stash them all over my body to get them back to camp. On this particular day, we don't have a complete strip search, but we have a search. We have to take our shirt off and lay everything out on the ground in front of us. We are only allowed to keep our skivvies on.

Not surprisingly, my buddy, Charlie Chaplin, shows up to do my inspection. He asks his usual question, "Tobacco?"

I say, "No, no tobacco." He discovers my stash and forces me to make a deal. I end up promising to give him 500 cigarettes. I get through the inspection and then hand the rest of the cigarettes over to my friend, Stanley Weisnewski, so he can hide them. He exclaims, "Hide them? Where the hell did you get all these cigarettes?" I tell him to keep 500 out to pay off the guard and hide the rest. An hour later, Charlie shows up to get his payoff and I give him a hundred cigarettes. He is as mad as a son-of-a-bitch.

I say, "If you don't take the hundred cigarettes, then they will probably catch me, and I'll have to tell them you were getting paid off." He took the hundred cigarettes.

At the camp, there are five of us that stick together. We trust each other implicitly. We share everything. I do most of the trading. They call me the cocan {exchanger} kid. My best friend is Harold "Pop" Lundberg from West Newbury, MA. The youngest guy in our group is Floyd Woodward. He is only nineteen years old. Stan "Ski" Weisnewski is the oldest. He is in his late thirties. Stan is always sick, so he stays in camp and takes care of the clothes, bedding, and finds places to stash our loot. He is a Chief Radioman with nearly twenty years of service. The other guy in our group is Red Christianson. He is the "jack of all trades" who salvaged the Scotch whiskey out of the capsized barge in the Philippines. Christianson had been a professional hockey player in Canada before the war. For some unknown reason, he migrated down to the state of Washington and enlisted in the Navy.

Weisnewski had tuberculosis while he was in the camp and most likely gave it to Woodward. After Woodward came back to the states, he also came down with TB. A lot of guys came down with it.

The five of us help each other to survive. We stick together all the way through.

There are other groups of guys who stand together, but I don't know that much about them because I am always concentrating on my group. I know about two brothers in camp who stick together, the Jaeger brothers. They came from DesMoines, Iowa. We call one "Senior" and the other one "Junior".

This camp has 500 enlisted men, of which 300 are Americans from all branches of the armed services. Most of the Americans are from the Navy. The other 200 are British, Canadian, Aussie, Norwegian, and Swedes. Guys from different nationalities tend to group together. We also have civilian internees. The most popular conversation at the camp is discussing what everyone is going to do after the war. Most of the POWs future plans involve food. We talk endlessly about what we are going to eat when we are freed from captivity. One POW explains that after he is freed, he is going to buy huge bags of rice and beans, go to an island by himself, and spend all his time eating. I can sympathize with his obsession with food, but I still think he is crazy.

We have fifty officers of all nationalities. About ten of them are American. Most of them keep to themselves and have nothing to do with us. The only officer we trust is a British officer named Major Tiesdale. The officers get preferential treatment as POWs. They do not have to work unless they volunteer. Some six of them do work. I understand they handle blueprints in the yard. Most of the time they sit around playing cards all day. According to International Law, they are not supposed to work officers.

However, any officers who give them a lot of problems are sent to a "special" camp, where they have to work. We have a Dutch doctor in our camp, who complains about the lack of medicine for POWs. He spends a lot of time at the camp commandant's office, trying to advocate for us. I see the little Dutchman standing at attention by the Japanese commandant's door, protesting the fact that the POWs have no access to medicinal supplies of any sort. He is a courageous man. He is sent to the "special" camp.

During all the time I am at the Yokohama camp, the POWs never receive any medical treatment. We never see so much as an aspirin. The only way you can get out of work is if you run a temperature of over one hundred. They used to take our temperatures under the arm. So, we used to take small test tube bottles, fill them with hot water, and put them under our armpits. When we visit the Japanese medic to get our temperatures taken, we covertly open our arms and let the bottle drop out without him seeing it. One time I have a temperature of 106. The medic says, "Oh, you are very sick!" and I get the day off. Everyone has some kind of gimmick to try to get a break from work. Some of the gimmicks worked and some didn't.

Our treatment often depended on the camp commandant. The Yokohama camp periodically changed commandants. One time, we got a Japanese officer who had lost a leg in Manchuria. He was the best commandant we had.

We are supposed to get a Red Cross package once a week, but we never do. All the time I am here, 40 months, I receive one Red Cross parcel, which has been looted of all the good things. I also receive a package from home, but that is it.

So, you can see that anyway you can supplement your diet helps. I still only weigh 100 pounds.

Often, they wake us up at night for a roll call {tinko}. While we stand outside, the Japs search our personal quarters and belongings. These sleep interruptions keep us in weakened conditions, and it goes on and on, week after week.

The Japanese run their trucks on charcoal. They use charcoal burners on the trucks because they don't have enough gasoline. There is a charcoal factory behind the prison camp in Yokohama. Someone broke a hole in the fence, so we have all the charcoal we want. We have pot-bellied stoves in the warehouse we are in. Of course, we don't have anything in the way of food to put in the stoves. Still, we load them up with charcoal to keep warm. Sometimes, Japanese guards come inside to warm their hands by the stoves, without knowing where the charcoal is coming from.

May, 1943. A dysentery epidemic breaks out in Yokohama. We have to give stool samples to test for this. I thought this was a good chance to get off work for a while. So, I use another POW's sample, who I thought had it. Sure enough, he did and I was taken off work and isolated with about fifty others in camp. For about a month we are isolated in a separate section of our camp. We are not allowed to have any contact or communication with anyone else in the camp.

I have a lot of free time on my hands, so I construct a crude cigarette-rolling machine. I had already obtained rice paper sheets from my job in the shipyard. I figured out how to cut them in half and use them to roll cigarettes. I recruit about ten guys to pick up used cigarette butts. They bring the butts to me, I strip them down, dry the tobacco in the sun, and then use the rice paper sheets to roll cigarettes. I pay the guys who gather the butts with fresh cigarettes. This kept me occupied for the month I spent in isolation at the camp.

Everything was okay until they ship us to a hospital camp in Shinagawa, a town just outside of Tokyo. This camp has about 300 POW's from the ten camps all over the Tokyo area. We can see Mount Fujiama from our location. There are huts with four rooms. Each room has twelve men. Everyday, we are given medicine, which we are supposed to self-inject. The American Army MD, Cap Weinstein {from Chelsea, MA}, tells us to throw the medicine away, which we do.

The food is about a cup of cooked grain and watery soup twice a day. Our ration comes from sweeping a warehouse near us. I know because I was on that detail and swept the floor for our rations once. The rice we eat is scattered all over the warehouse floor. It is mixed with dirt, rat dung, and anything else that fell on the floor. We clean the dirt and rat dung out of the rice and eat it. I weigh myself when I am in the warehouse. I am 75 pounds. One of the most important parts of our diet is our bone ration. We get bones from a slaughterhouse and make soup with what is given to us. We are on a bone list, and I can't wait for my turn. We crack the bones open and eat the marrow. Two guys started fighting once over a bone. They almost beat each other to death and we had to break them up.

Every night, we are forced to sing patriotic Japanese songs. Of course, we change the wording a bit. Some of the changes include such poetic phrases like "Fuck the Japanese" and so on. We keep up a good façade, so they never catch on to our subtle lyrical alterations.

Fall, 1943. Five months later, we are sent back to our work camp in Yokohama. I can just about walk and this is the time I almost had it. My buddies in the camp give me part of their rations when I first arrive. It helps me a lot. The garbage at work is also a welcome addition and I put some weight back on. I never do get over 100 pounds again. When I met my brother, Walter, in Oakland, CA, I had put on about 20 pounds in two weeks. My body was like a sponge.

One day, I am at the pier loading coke onto my pushcart to bring it back to the pipe shop. I see a German sailor walk by. German raiders used to operate out of the Indian Ocean. When they captured a ship, they used to bring it to Tokyo because it was too far to bring it all the way back to Germany.

The German sailor spoke to me in perfect English. He said, "It doesn't look like they're feeding you guys too much, are they?"

I said, "No, we're not getting much."

He couldn't get too close because he didn't want the Japanese to know he was talking to me.

Discreetly, he said, "Tomorrow, when you come down for your supply of coke, look under the pile and I'll have something there for you."

The next day, I go down there and I find a large pig hidden under the pile of coke. The pig is frozen solid. I figured he must have stolen it from a large walk-in freezer on his ship.

I bring the pig back to the pipe shop in the pushcart. I place it in one of the large furnaces and cook it up. I pass on the word to the other Americans in the pipe shop. The guys meet me in the shop and I cut huge slabs of meat for them. We have a feast. The Japanese workers in the shop have never seen a pig before, so they thought it wasn't fit to eat. When we had all eaten as much as we could, I drained all the fat out of the cooked pig and put it into bottles. I hide the bottles in my clothes and bring them back to camp. We are starved for fat in our diets, so we use the bottles to sprinkle some fat onto our rice every morning.

Winter of 1943-1944. We work at the shipyard all winter with very little rest or time off. Most of the Japanese workers are now of the opinion that they will lose the war, but not for quite a while yet. My co-worker, Tanabai, helps me a lot by dealing with me. He says, "American good. Nippon damn." He believes me no matter what I tell him. Of course, some of it is baloney, but we Americans are a bragging race anyway.

In 1944, the Japs build a bathtub measuring 15'x15'x 4' in one of the warehouses in our camp. Before that, we only got an occasional improvised shower by pouring cold water on ourselves. We never had any soap. We take turns in the bath once a week. Every week they fill it up with hot water. We have numbers we go by. This group would go in first, and then this group, and so on. The ones that came up last, 25 at a time, had some dirty water. There was scum floating on the water a half-inch thick. I never took a bath as long as I was there. I bathed at work once in a while. I also washed my clothes at work.

The current Mitsubishi boss is no damn good. He asks me to shave him one day. I do, but all the time I am tempted to slit his throat. Then later, I shave myself on the job, unknown to him. He later finds out and gets pissed, but I just ignore him. He's a working bastard, but in many ways I impede his production. although it puts more labor on me. Oh well, I'm in good shape now and I don't give a damn.

Okamoto {"Silver"}, the interpreter for the guards, has done his best to make us as comfortable as possible. Okamoto lived in the U.S. for twenty years, working as a perfume salesman. When the war broke out, he returned to Japan. He could speak English as well as any of us. He's probably a spy and is acting as an interpreter to divert attention from what his actual duty is. Most of the time I'm too weak to have any sex drive, but Okamoto has a damn good-looking daughter who I'd like to go a few fast rounds with.

Spring, 1944. In spring, a young man's fancy turns to love. Oh, yes, it seems I've heard that before, but that was before Pearl Harbor. The boys {American POW's} rob the Japs blind, out-trade them, and sabotage them whenever they can. I throw nuts and bolts into a big diesel crankcase, break a gas line, and break an airline. Some of the boys put wooden plugs in the pipes to stop them up. The Japanese would install the pipes in their ships, the pipes would get stopped up, and they would have to take them all apart to fix them. The war work has slacked off tremendously in the last few weeks, but that is mainly because no new ships have been launched. It takes them at least six months to build a tanker and a year to build a seaplane tender. It is poor work at best. When are the boys {American soldiers} coming to this dump? If they only knew what we prisoners know. The

Japs haven't got anything to speak of and no modern equipment. Their transportation system could be knocked out with a few well-placed bombs.

Summer, 1944. The normal routine of beatings, night stand-ups, and punishments occur when the least little excuse offers itself. As things are going bad for them in the war, the guards get worse. We have nicknames for all of them. The Japs on my list include "Kotex", "Pretty Boy", "Bat Eye", "Bulldog", "Black Sleeves", "the Co", "Suzuki", "Gertie", "Liver Lips", "Crook-shank", "Super-stripe", "Horai", and all the Jap army guards and foos not mentioned here.

During the summer of 1944, the Japanese began moving all their prisoners to Japan. As the American forces closed in, the Japanese retreated from the Pacific islands on ships, taking their prisoners with them. We weren't aware of it at the time, but thousands of POWs were being inadvertently killed as our forces sank the Japanese transports they were on. American POW, Hank Henderson, was one of the prisoners who were transported out of the Philippines on "hell-ships" in the summer of '44. He described his experience in his diary:

> August 14, 1944. We came in from work and were told to line up in two ranks, ten paces apart. The first rank was told to go inside the barracks and pack our gear, we were going back to Bilibid in Manila. There were 309 POWs in camp. Nine were classified as sick and the other one hundred and fifty were in the first rank with me. We marched down to the Japanese transport and went aboard. Little known to us, Admiral Halsey's seventh fleet of carriers and Admiral Spruance's submarines were sinking almost all shipping and all war crafts in the Philippines. We continued to work from the hold of the ship for the next month. {Henderson, PT 1, p.5}

Hank Henderson and his fellow POWs were transported to Manila on September 18th, 1944, where they were held again in Bilibid Prison. The American forces were bombing Manila, so some of the POWs in the prison were injured from nearby bomb hits. Other POW survivors of Japanese transports, which were sunk by our forces, were brought to Bilibid, so they could wait to be shipped out again on other transports. On October 1st, 1944, Hank Henderson and his fellow POWs boarded a transport to begin the deadly journey to Japan. They were packed tightly into a lower hold with no ventilation. Mr. Henderson describes a close call he experienced a week into the journey:

> October 8, 1944. The northern coast of Luzon, Philippines Islands. This is my birthday. We were in a convoy of ten ships heading for Japan. Late in the afternoon, an oil tanker off our starboard bow was struck by a torpedo. It

was so close to us, the spray and debris was strewn on the decks of our ship. God it looked like the end was at long last in sight. We were all so miserable, many of us welcomed the chance to end it all by going to the bottom with the ship, because we already knew it was impossible for us to get out of the hold of the ship if it was sunk. {Henderson, PT 1, p.6}

Hank Henderson was at sea on a hell-ship from October 1st, 1944 to November 9th, 1944. He and the other POWs were brought to a camp in Formosa {Taiwan} where they worked at a farm and a sugar mill until late January. On January 25th, 1945 they were forced to board yet another hell-ship so they could be transported to mainland Japan. Mr. Henderson traveled on another transport from January 25th, 1945 to February 14th, 1945, until they finally arrived in Moji, Japan. From there, he and the other POWs were transported by train to Kawasaki, which was across the river from Tokyo, where the POWs were forced to work in a heavy manufacturing plant. It was all a matter of luck whether a POW transport made it to Japan. As the American attacks escalated, the POW's luck became steadily worse.

As I mentioned before, our guards get worse as the war goes badly for them. One time, a Japanese guard sees me take a potato from a storage area and tells his superior.

They bring me to an interrogation room and ask, "Where is the potato?"

I deny taking it so they begin beating me. I continue to deny it and they continue beating me. During the beatings, they never stop asking where the potato is. The potato was in my pocket the whole time. They never searched me.

After the beatings, they throw me in a cell for five days. I eat the evidence in the cell when they aren't looking. My jaw was broken, so I couldn't open my mouth fully for four months. I could open my mouth barely enough to eat and drink, but it was very painful. Eventually, it got better. I could open my jaw fully again after several months.

We hear about an American POW named Harris, who goes berserk at his job in the shipyard and uses an iron bar to beat some Japanese workers senseless. No one was killed. The Jap guards subdued him and turned him over to the civilian authorities. They didn't put him in a prisoner of war camp. They shipped him to a civilian Japanese prison, where he was placed in permanent solitary confinement. He survived. At the end of the war, the American forces found him in the Japanese prison. I believe he avoided execution because the Mitsubishi Corporation didn't want a black mark on their record after the war was over.

Mitsubishi LTD has done the minimum to ease our situation. Here they are, a big, profitable outfit, and they are going to pay through the nose for what they've done to us. The personnel supervisor in the shipyard was Udo San {Mr. Udo}. If it wasn't for Udo San, our lot would be hopeless. He's nearly as American as I because he spent some time in the U.S. He worked for Mitsubishi in the United States for many years. He had an American wife and three kids back in the states. He did as much as he could for us.

When President Roosevelt dies on April 12th, 1945, Udo San assembles three hundred of us in front of a podium before we go back to the camp at the end of the workday. He informs us that President Roosevelt has died and says, "Anyone who wants to wear a black armband, I have them here in this box."

None of us took a black armband. We figured Roosevelt was the son-of-a-bitch who put us in that position by getting us into the war and not backing us up in the Philippines.

I always figured Roosevelt and Churchill let Pearl Harbor happen. It couldn't have been any other way. It was the only way to get us into the European war. There were many warning signs that the Pearl Harbor attack was going to happen, which were blatantly ignored. There were a number of blunders made, but the attack on Pearl Harbor was obvious. Did it make any sense to send the fleet out from Long Beach, California, where they were safe, and relocate them to Hawaii in the middle of the Pacific, where they were exposed and vulnerable? At the time, the U.S. had a boycott on giving the Japanese oil and steel. Before the embargo, the Japanese were using our fuel for their ships. If they couldn't get our fuel, they were out of business. They had to knock our fleet out to keep their war effort going. They needed to go down to the Dutch East Indies and get the oil down there. The Japanese were negotiating in Washington to stop the oil and steel embargo at the same time they attacked Pearl Harbor. Obviously, their negotiations were all a big hoax.

Who were the top guys in Washington who allowed Pearl Harbor to happen? There are many theories. Roosevelt's top military advisors at the time were Secretary of War, Henry Stimson, Secretary of the Navy, Frank Knox, Chief of Naval Operations, Admiral Stark {the same guy who got me out of mess duty on the U.S.S. Cincinatti}, Assistant Chief of Naval Operations, Rear Admiral Royal Ingersol, and the Chief of Staff of the U.S. Army, General George Marshall. These men were part of Roosevelt's inner military circle and were privy to all the information obtained by the American Code-breakers. Like FDR, they all knew about the imminent threat from Japan and failed to warn the Commander-in-Chief of the Pacific fleet at Pearl Harbor, Admiral Kimmel. The Assistant Chief of Naval Operations, Admiral Ingersol, ordered the Code-breaking station in Corregidor, station CAST, to provide intercepts to Admiral Hart and General MacArthur, but not to Admiral Kimmel at Pearl Harbor.

A memo was written in October, 1940 by the head of the Far East Desk of the Office of Naval Intelligence, Lieutenant Commander Arthur H. McCollum. McCollum's memo outlined eight specific steps that could be taken by the United States to provoke Japan into war. McCollum had lived in Japan for a number of years and was an expert in Japanese psychology. The eight steps constituted a form of psychological warfare against Japan, which was intended to anger and offend their military government into attacking the United States. All the steps were put into effect by the Roosevelt administration before the Pearl Harbor attack.

McCollum's first step to provoke Japan was called Action A, which called for making an agreement with Britain to use their Pacific bases, including Singapore. This was put into effect by the Roosevelt administration. Action B was making an agreement with Holland to use their bases and obtain supplies from the Dutch East Indies. This was done. Action C was giving aid to Chiang Kai Chek's Chinese government. Done. Action D was sending two submarine divisions to the Orient. I personally know this was done because I served as one of the crew of the submarine, U.S.S. Permit, which was part of the submarine fleet sent to the Orient. Action G was making an agreement with the Dutch East Indies to start an oil embargo on Japan. Done. One of the most important steps in the memo, Action H, was the oil and steel embargo initiated against Japan by the United States and Britain. Done. Another important step in the memo, Action F, was moving the U.S. Fleet from California to Pearl Harbor, Hawaii. Done.

The commander of the Pacific fleet, Admiral Richardson, objected to moving the fleet into Hawaiian waters because of the inherent danger of attack. Richardson made numerous objections to placing the fleet at Pearl Harbor and was overruled by President Roosevelt every time. On February 1st, 1941, Roosevelt fired Admiral Richardson and replaced him with Admiral Husband E. Kimmel. Richardson was re-assigned to a relatively unimportant desk job in Washington. Kimmel was kept completely out of the intelligence loop, so he never received any information from the American Code-breakers.

The Director of Naval Intelligence, Captain Walter Anderson, was loyal to Roosevelt. On April 1st, 1940 Roosevelt promoted Captain Anderson to rear admiral and assigned him the command of the Pacific Fleet battleships. It was widely believed that Anderson was not qualified for the job. It was rumored he was given the job because he agreed with Roosevelt's provocation policies toward

Japan. Anderson was brought into Roosevelt's military clique and was privy to all the information retrieved by the American Code-breakers, including the movement of the main Japanese battle fleet toward Hawaii. He knew about the strong potential for an imminent attack, but he never passed on the information to the commander at Pearl Harbor, Admiral Kimmel. All but one of Admiral Anderson's battleships were destroyed in the Pearl Harbor attack. The only surviving battleship had been moved to the West Coast.

By 1941, the American Code-breakers had decoded all the major Japanese codes. Code-breakers had solved the Japanese diplomatic code, known as Purple, and the Japanese Five-Number military codes. The American Code-breakers had intercepted Japanese messages describing the movement of the main Japanese battle fleet toward Hawaii. They had also intercepted diplomatic messages describing the Japanese deadline for the initiation of hostilities; 7:30am on December 7th, 1941, Hawaiian time. Ironically, some of the Code-breakers were stationed at Pearl Harbor. If they had been allowed to walk down the hall and talk to somebody in charge, they could have warned them about what was about to happen. All decoded messages had to go through Washington first. As mentioned, Washington never passed on the decoded messages to the commander at Pearl Harbor, Admiral Kimmel. The results were that Pearl Harbor was devastated by a surprise attack and the nation became united to go into the European war and the Pacific war.

The problem is that the leaders of countries don't give a damn about the little guy. The leaders of our country, who let Pearl Harbor happen, didn't expect that the Japanese would cause as much damage as they did. To say that they underestimated the Japanese attack is a severe understatement. The bottom line is that a conscious decision was made by some of our leaders to sacrifice a number of young men's lives in order to bring our country into the European war sooner.

I spoke with some of the Navy Code-breakers on Corregidor. Each radioman was assigned to monitor a specific Japanese ship. During the week before Pearl Harbor, most radio communications in the main Japanese fleet went silent. In warfare, radio silence is interpreted to mean an enemy is up to something; planning an attack. Some important top-level Japanese communications were still sent in the midst of the overall radio silence. These top-level instructions, related to the Pearl Harbor attack, were intercepted by American Code-breakers, which revealed the movement of the main Japanese battle fleet toward Hawaii. Why were these intercepts not sent to the commander of the Pacific fleet at Pearl Harbor, Admiral Kimmel? The entire Asiatic fleet had been put on a Condition Three Alert, which meant attack was imminent. Why were we prepared to be attacked, but Pearl Harbor wasn't? Was our communication network so poor that we couldn't get a message from the Philippines to Hawaii? The only explanation is that it must have been a setup.

We have a U.S Navy Radio Code-man in our camp in Yokohama. He was the guy the Japs were searching for at the camp in Formosa. The Japanese try hard to find him, but they never do. He is in the camp under an assumed name. Eventually, with our help, he is able to build a short wave radio set that picks up all the news from San Francisco. We scavenged the parts he used to build the radio from our various shipyard jobs. During our first year at the camp in 1942, the word went around for POWs to pick up any kind of radio parts they could at their jobs. I had access to a storeroom where they kept the supplies for the pipe shop. There was a small American-made radio on the shelf, so I took the radio, hid it under my clothes, and brought it back to camp. I turned it in to the Radio Code-man.

Only the officers received the news right away. They usually waited about a month to disseminate the news throughout the general camp. They figured if everyone was talking about the latest news, then the Japanese would get wise to what we were doing.

When are the air-raids going to start? The sooner the better. I know this place will get it, but that will do my heart good. We are aware of the progress of the Naval war in the Pacific from American pilots who are taken prisoner from time to time. Sometimes we receive an English edition of the Nippon Times. All we have to do is turn the news around 180 degrees and that turns out to be the truth.

12

Air Raids

Around Thanksgiving day in 1944, an air raid alarm goes off at about noontime. Several other POW's and myself are outside and we look up to see four very high vapor trails. We watch a Jap fighter plane diving on a B-29 bomber, but it misses. We now figure the end of the war is near.

On February 22, 1945, early one morning, American dive-bombers appear. They bomb Yokohama Bay and sink five ships, one of which is an aircraft carrier. On March 8 and 9, 1945, the B-29's fly overhead starting at 10pm. We can see the sky aglow in the distance. An hour later, the main force comes over and sets everything on fire from Yokohama to Tokyo, a distance of 25 miles.

Hank Henderson was working at the Kawasaki plant outside of Tokyo when the bombing raids occurred on March 8 and 9. The plant where he worked was a prime target. He described the bombing attacks in his diary:

> March 8-9, 1945 11:00-01:30 hrs. USAAF General LeMay's B-29 incendiary bombing of Tokyo and Kawasaki consisted of three hundred and thirty four of these large Super-Forts. We were right in the middle of all this planned arson. Eighty three thousand people were killed and over forty thousand injured, plus total destruction of a large part of the cities. A gale type wind was also blowing, fanning the fires as they burned. It is utterly unbelievable the amount of destruction and loss of life a fire storm of this magnitude can cause. The plant where I worked, Kagaku {formerly Suzuki}, was totally destroyed. It appears these planes come so close to the ground, we could talk to the air crewmen. The more we yelled, the more they bombed us. Boy, did they have fun. You could say there was a hot time in the old town that night. It was this area, not Hiroshima or Nagasaki, where the most loss of life and destruction took place. {Henderson, PT 2, p.1}

The B-29's flew in single-file. I later found out they took all the guns off the B-29's so they could carry more incendiary bombs. That meant they couldn't fire back when they were attacked. The B-29's flew extremely low for more effective bombing. They flew in a formation about a mile apart. The Japanese would concentrate their searchlights on every third plane and try to shoot it down. A Japanese fighter plane, with its landing lights on, would fly behind the B-29 and fire into the right inboard engine. This caused the B-29 to explode. I saw three of them explode in mid-air. Some B-29's were shot down over the ocean. We had five submarines outside of Tokyo harbor to pick up anyone who was able to get out of the planes.

We saw one B-29 fly directly over our camp about one hundred feet high in a ball of flame. We thought he was going to hit our camp. I never did find out how he made out. The Japanese said they shot down 200 of our B-29s during that air raid. We saw 28 B-29s shot down just in our area, so their claim may have been accurate.

Two days later, we go back to work. Everything surrounding the shipyard is gone. Most of the buildings outside the shipyard have been reduced to rubble. The shipyard itself was hardly touched. I figured they must have had some kind of intelligence that we POWs were working in the shipyard. Also, our POW camp was never hit by any bombs. There were a few close hits nearby, but none inside the camp.

One day, I am taking a break from work with a Japanese co-worker. While we are talking, I discover the thing the Japanese people are most afraid of. Apparently, the thing that frightened the Japanese more than anything was the U.S. Marines. There was a lot of propaganda circulating in Japan that the Marines were ruthless bastards.

My Japanese co-worker asked me, "When the Marines come, what are they going to do?"

I said, "When the Marines come, you better stay inside the house." I explained, "the Marines are all six feet, six inches tall and carry two swords, one in each hand," I added that, "they would come in swinging their swords like whirlwinds, chopping people's heads off."

I asked my Japanese co-worker how he made out in the big bombing raid. He said, "Three years ago, my relatives out in the country told me to get out of the big city. They said that someday the Americans are going to bomb the cities and I will lose my life. So, I moved out of the city."

My co-worker moved into the country and it took him two hours to get to work. Still, he told me, "I'm glad I made that decision."

Before the bombing raids, the Japanese cut huge swathes, 200 yards wide, throughout the cities of Yokohama and Tokyo. They knocked all the houses down in the swathe areas, so the fires wouldn't spread all over the city. When the B-29's flew over, we could see the bombs dropping. The incendiary bombs hit the ground, blew apart, and hundreds of canisters of jelly gasoline flew out, igniting many fires. There was no defense against them. The swathes did very little to stop the spread of fires.

The Japanese said they lost 100,000 people in the bombing raids, but it had to have been a lot more. Many people lived in shacks, one on top of the other, in thick clusters.

When the bombs started hitting, they would try to seek refuge in the water and they got boiled to death. That's what war is all about. It's terrible. I think about 500,000 people may have lost their lives in those bombing raids.

Then, during late March, we are at work when we are ordered out of the shipyard to the area outside the yard. We watch 125 B-29's fly over in formation, led by a B-24. I know there are 125 planes because I count them in the sky. They fly in groups of nine. They drop leaflets and fly on unopposed. Now, we know it is almost over! No bombs were dropped!

As the situation becomes more precarious for the Japanese, the C.O. {Commanding Officer} transfers us out of the shipyard and sends us up to the Yokohama Country Club. This is the first time I have been on a golf course. We are rolling up the fairways and making farms for growing food.

Late March, 1945. While at the golf course, the air raid alarm goes off. The Jap guards take shelter in the trenches. We look up and see two American P-51 fighter planes flying between the clouds. We see two Jap fighters take off about a mile away. The two P-51's fly down and shoot the Jap fighters down.

One P-51 flies right over us at about 100 feet. We run out with our shirts off and wave. He wobbles his wings and flies on. AA fire is bursting right behind him. Great day now—we know we have a base close to Japan! Shortly after that, we are moved to Tokyo by train.

We didn't know it at the time, but the Marines had declared the island of Iwo Jima secure on March 26, 1945, after more than a month of heavy fighting. Iwo Jima was only 650 miles from mainland Japan and was under the jurisdiction of the Tokyo government. The first group of Marines invaded the island at 09:00 on February 19th, 1945. The Japanese had an elaborate underground complex on the island consisting of more than 1500 underground rooms and over sixteen miles of tunnels. The island of Iwo Jima had received the most intense aerial and Naval bombardment at that time in the Pacific War. The bombardment had little effect because most of the Japanese forces and equipment were hidden in underground bunkers. The Marines landing on the beach were caught in an intense crossfire from machine gunners and artillery, firing from underground positions. The Marines couldn't see their enemy, but their enemy had a clear view of them.

The Marines advanced through sheets of gunfire, taking heavy casualties. Pure determination and heroism kept the Marines moving forward through intense gunfire and artillery fire being launched at them from unseen underground enemies. The Japanese defenders considered the island to be sacred Japanese soil and were ordered to fight to the death. Only 200 Japanese POWs were taken out of 22,000 soldiers defending the island. At the end of the battle, the Marines had suffered 26,000 casualties with nearly 7000 soldiers dead. Over a quarter of the Medals of Honor awarded to the Marines in World War II were given for heroic conduct during the invasion of Iwo Jima.

As the battle for Iwo Jima was ending in late March, the battle for Okinawa was just beginning. The island of Okinawa was strategically located between the southernmost island of Japan, Kyushu, and Formosa, which is now modern Taiwan. Okinawa was only 375 miles from mainland Japan. Unlike Iwo Jima, Okinawa was the home of a civilian population estimated at about 300,000 people. Okinawa was the site of the largest amphibious landing and the last major battle in the Pacific War. More people were killed in the battle of Okinawa than during the atomic bomb attacks on Hiroshima and Nagasaki. Total American casualties were estimated at 12,000 killed and 36,000 wounded. The Navy experienced huge losses; almost 5000 men killed in battle. The Marines and the Army lost about 8,000 men fighting on the island. Total Japanese casualties numbered more than 100,000 killed in the fighting, almost 24,000 sealed in caves, and more than 10,000 captured or surrendered. The Army estimated the total number of civilian casualties to be at least 130,000; more than one third of the total population of Okinawa. Many of these civilian casualties resulted from suicide prompted by the fear of the U.S. Marines. The Japanese propaganda machine had described the Marines as ruthless killers who tortured civilians. Many civilians believed this myth and killed themselves, rather than be captured.

In mid-march, 1945, an American fleet of more than 1300 ships assembled off the coast of Okinawa to start the Naval bombardment. On March 18th, 1945, the Japanese began launching their deadly kamikaze or "suicide plane attacks" on American ships. On April 1st, 1945, the land invasion of Okinawa began when 60,000 U.S. Marines and Army soldiers landed on the island. During the first day of the landing, the American fleet launched the heaviest concentration of Naval bombardment ever to support an amphibious landing. On April 6th and 7th, the first massive formations of hundreds of kamikaze aircraft was launched against the American fleet. A total of 1,465 kamikaze fighters sank 30 American ships and damaged 164 others. The American forces lost 763 aircraft. The Japanese lost 7,830 aircraft and 16 warships. The battle for Okinawa lasted from April 1st, 1945 to June 29th, 1945. Even before the battle was over, the island of Okinawa was being prepared by U.S. work crews to be the launching point for a massive invasion of the Japanese home islands, known as "Operation Downfall".

In early May, 1945, the Japanese decide to transfer us to Tokyo by train. They had built an elevated train system that traveled from Yokohama to Tokyo. When we ride the train, we see that everything on either side of the tracks had been completely burnt out. As far as we can see from left to right, everything is gone. The only things left standing are an occasional brick building or steel structure. The American bombing raids had inflicted massive damage all the way from Yokohama to Tokyo.

Headquarters Camp "Omari", Tokyo-about May 9th or 10th, 1945. The camp is on an island accessible only on foot on a 4' wide bridge 100 yards long. The island was built by British POW's early in the war. It is about a half-mile long and a quarter-mile wide. High-ranking Japs being tried for war crimes were kept here later.

During the massive bombing raids of March 8th and 9th, minimal damage was done to the POW camp. They only lost two buildings and part of their bridge from the raids. Everything on shore was destroyed. We picked up unexploded firebombs all over the island after the raid. The unexploded firebombs looked like welding rod canisters. Many life rafts drifted ashore, which meant many B-29's had been shot down.

At this camp Omari, most of the POW's were British and they worked in the railroad yard loading and unloading freight. They had everything they needed and they lived very well, food-wise. They didn't share though!

I get to know a sailor who had been shot down over Iwo Jima in 1942 during one of the Navy's hit-and-run raids at that time. Robert Tant is his name, from Alabama. He has a plan all worked out to get extra food. He is a daring guy and I go along with his plan.

While the camp is putting on a show tonight, we are going to carry out our raid. He goes over it with me and in the daytime we make a dummy run. We go to the warehouse storing rice and grain, which is surrounded by a high wooden fence. The Japs had placed tin cans all over this area to keep POW's out, thinking that the noise would deter us in case we tried to get something.

Tant and I move into this area, which is unguarded in the daytime but under guard at night. He and I make stepping places by moving the noisy cans out of the way in certain spots. We count our steps to where the rice is stored and pull a board from the wall to get at the rice. We had made tubes out of bamboo that were about a foot long with the separations knocked out. There was too much traffic in and out of the warehouse during the daytime, so we decided nighttime was our best chance.

The night of the big camp party, we tie our pants at the ankles; this is to be our storage for the rice. When we get to the area, we sneak by the guard, who is distracted by the show. We move cautiously to the storage buildings and slip the bamboo contraptions into the rice bags. We fill our pants up with as much rice as they can hold.

The only thing we miscalculated on was the bulk that the rice created in our pants. We can hardly bend our legs. Because of this, we make a lot of noise, but the guard is still intently watching the show, so we get away with the raid. When we arrive back in the barracks, we place the rice in bags and hide them. We had these hiding places planned in advance.

Another POW was an expert at making hot plates by using clay and resistance wire. Where he obtained these materials God only knows. He demanded half the rice that he cooked on the plates. Everyone had a scam going, it seemed.

I only spent three weeks at this camp and I hated to leave, as I was eating well. Another building contained Red Cross boxes, which we were supposed to be receiving but never did. My friend had a plan to raid this warehouse, but I was transferred before it came off. I never did find out how he made out. Tant was only 19years old at the time. He was a Radioman Gunner on a TBF plane.

13

Liberation

Early June, 1945. I am one of three hundred Americans transferred to north Honshu to a town in the mountains about fifty miles from the coast of Sendai. Honshu is the main island in Japan. The railway comes to a dead-end high in the mountains in the town of Wakasaning {pop. 500}.

Mitsubishi owned everything in Japan with four other families. Here, they owned iron ore mines and a smelter fired by electricity. This is where we worked. It was about two miles from our camp, which was brand new. It's possible that Mitsubishi wanted to transfer us to a safer location so they could be on the good side of the American occupation forces when the war was over. At this time, the handwriting was on the wall. The unopposed formation of 125 American B-29's led by a single B-24, dropping propaganda leaflets, probably helped to convince them.

In early June, Hank Henderson was also transferred to a new camp. He describes his experience in his diary:

> June 1, 1945, 08:00 hrs. You guessed it, another march. This would be our last move. We were transferred to the Tokyo War Prisoner's Camp number one. We continued working at Kagaku, doing salvage and cleanup work on the premises. {Henderson, PT 2, p.2}

We know the war is just about over. Our concern is "what are they going to do with us?"

We knew a long time ago that we were slated to be killed if an invasion happened. An order had been issued by the Japanese high command to execute all POWs the moment the first American soldiers stepped foot on mainland Japan. The camp commandants were allowed to choose their own methods of execution. We prepare as much as we can for our inevitable executions. I make a knife notched on the end, so I can tie it onto a pole and use it as a spear.

Another American POW has a .45 caliber pistol. How was he able to keep and maintain this weapon? At that time, we used to make our own soap. The American POW took the separate parts of his .45 automatic pistol and hid them in various pieces of soap. When he put all the pieces together, he had a workable .45. We are planning to rush the guards and take over the camp, if they try to kill us in the event of an American invasion.

We work in a smelting plant where they smelted iron ore down to pig iron, which is the first stage of making steel. My job is directing the molten iron to the molds that we made in the sand in front of two blast furnaces. After that was done, I have to shovel the sludge out of the pit next to the furnaces. I'm amazed how hard I could work then at 100 pounds, when now at 165 pounds I can do so little.

On July 9th, 1945, I am working in front of the furnace when I see sparks shooting from the base of the furnaces. I tap my guard on the shoulder and ask him what was going on. He started to run out of the building and I wasn't far behind.

The furnace blows up and that is the last thing I can remember until I wake up three or four days later in camp. We have an American Army Doctor named Captain Salavar. He asks me what my name is. I answer him by saying, "I'm hungry."

But boy, what a headache I have. After eating and drinking some tea, I try to get up, but I can't. It takes me a couple of days before I can get to a sitting position. Then, it is like learning to walk all over again.

Every day my friend, Harold "Pop" Lundberg, comes in and shakes me up, saying "You are part of my group. We need you. We need you because you are a good trader."

If he didn't come to see me every day like that, I was almost ready to say "the hell with it" and give up.

It seems the explosion knocked a plank out of the overhead and it landed on my head. It's a good thing it hit me there. Us Swedes are often called "hardheaded".

It is July 13th, 1945 and I am on the sick list until August 14th, 1945. I am supposed to go to work the next day. My shift, the day shift, is lined up on August 15th. Then, I see the graveyard shift come through the gates. There is no roll call {tinko} for them. The war is over. Our guards disappear that day and we POW's take over the camp. The only Japs left are the commander and a sergeant to account for all of us in the camp. The American occupation force in Tokyo sends out a radio message to the surrendering Japanese forces, telling them they better account for all their prisoners. They state in the message that if any prisoners are missing or killed, the Japanese officers will be held accountable and punished severely.

Hank Henderson's Tokyo camp was also liberated on August 15th, 1945. He describes the experience in his diary:

> August 15, 1945, 12:00 hrs. Over 1700 carrier borne planes plus a whole sky full of Super-Forts blacked out the sky. We were told to sit down and the Emperor of Japan had a message for the Nation. When he started speaking, we understood what he was saying. He told us Japan had lost the war and was to resist no longer. We marched back to the camp, and strangely enough, the next morning the Japanese guards were no longer in our camp. {Henderson, PT 2, p.2}

The Emperor had declared that the war was over, so the people listened to him. The military had tried to stop the Emperor from speaking and failed. The Japanese people had been under a military regime for the past hundred years, so they had no experience of freedom or thinking for themselves. The average Japanese person knew nothing, except for what they were told. That's why they never surrendered. They were ordered by their superiors not to surrender and they did everything they were ordered to do. They fought until they were killed. Only the word of the Emperor could override the orders of their military commanders.

For the Japanese warrior culture, a prisoner was the lowest form of life on earth. In western civilization, you fight each other and when you run out of ammunition, you give up and the other side treats you according to the rules of war. This was a completely alien concept to the Japanese. When I was first taken prisoner, I never expected to last more than a couple of days. I thought they were going to kill us all immediately. A short time later, they actually did try to kill us by gross negligence when they starved us for eighteen days in the Philippines. They tried to work and starve us to death. That was the name of the game. They did a pretty good job of it. The Japanese took approximately 28,000 American prisoners, most of them in the Philippines. Only 14,000 American POWs came back. Of the 14,000 that survived, there were 3000 that were blind from malnutrition. Most of them regained their eyesight after returning to the states.

Even the Japanese fighting style contrasted sharply with the western rules of warfare. By way of comparison, German soldiers would not intentionally shoot any soldier wearing a red cross on their helmet, which indicated he was a medic. German pilots wouldn't bomb tents marked with a red cross, signifying it as a hospital. Americans followed the same rules. To the western mind, it was a question of fairness and honor. It was not fair or honorable to kill a patient in a hospital. The Japanese saw it completely differently. The Japanese were trained to aim first at any soldiers wearing a red cross on their helmet. They figured that way, more American soldiers would die if they didn't receive medical treatment right away. American medics stopped wearing crosses on their helmets because they were getting targeted by Japanese snipers. After taking the crosses off their helmets, the America medics could only be distinguished from other soldiers by the medical pack they carried across their chest. When the Japanese figured this out, they trained their soldiers to prioritize killing any American soldiers seen wearing a medical pack. The Japanese artillery also prioritized the destruction of hospitals. Any tent with a cross on it was a priority target. This distinction in fighting tactics made the Japanese soldiers barbaric to western soldiers.

After getting word that the war was over, some guys go into town and get sick on green saki. I stay put. At this time I am as weak as a kitten. The next day, three Navy TBF's fly over and drop supplies. We place whitewashed doors on the parade grounds, so they can see where to make the drop. The parade grounds are 100' long and 50' wide. Like fools, we all stand around while the first one comes in. The plane drops two sea bags and one of them knocks a small building down. We all go inside after we see that drop.

The planes were from the carrier, U.S.S. Hancock. The sea bags contained candy bars, cigarettes, and most importantly, newspapers from all over the United States. The best present I could have received was news from home. Wow, how well I remember that day!

The next day, two B-17's fly over and drop two pallets, but they overshoot us and we never find a thing. We are located in a valley surrounded by mountains, so it is difficult to make an exact drop. Apparently, when the supplies were dropped, the parachutes didn't open and the boxes fell into the mountains. Over the radio, we are told to stay in the camp and await contact by our forces. Boy, we are getting restless. On August 19th, 1945, a man from the Swedish consulate arrives and tells us about the A-bomb that ended the war.

Truman's decision to drop the atomic bomb has always been considered controversial. The massive casualties inflicted on American forces during the battle of Okinawa helped Truman to make his decision. It was projected there would be more than a million American casualties if the United States invaded Japan. The bottom line is that we POWs owe our lives to Truman's decision to drop the atomic bombs. It was a well-known plan that the Japanese were going to kill all of us the moment the first American soldiers stepped foot on the main Japanese islands. The atomic bombs caused an immediate shock factor, which didn't give the Japanese time to systematically kill all of us. A group of thirty POWs being held in the vicinity of Hiroshima were murdered by the enraged Japanese survivors after the bomb annihilated the city. Thousands of us would have been systematically executed if our forces had invaded Japan.

We stay at the camp until August 29th, 1945 when we take over the train and go to the port of Sendai about fifty miles away in the northern province of Honshu. A LST is waiting to pick us up.

I'll never forget sitting up on the bow of the ship and overhearing a conversation between two sailors. One sailor said, "I have enough points to get out. Boy, I'm really glad to get out of here because I've been here for eight months!" I figured that after what I'd been through, I wouldn't have noticed eight months.

There is a short trip out to the hospital ship, U.S.S. Rescue. Before boarding, we are told to throw away everything we don't want. Most of us go aboard naked except for a G-string. I have a small diary that I kept hidden. I walk aboard the U.S.S. rescue with a diary and a G-string. I had the diary for a while, but I don't know whatever happened to it.

I have bites all over my body, from all the bugs. We weren't able to bathe while we were in the camp. We all had lice. The first thing we do is to have a delousing shower. Then, we have our first physical exams. As standard procedure, the Navy puts a tag on you that read: Diagnosis-Mild Malnutrition. I weigh about 85 pounds at the time. My normal weight is 180 pounds. Then, we have our first U.S. food in nearly four years. Strange as it may seem, I'm not hungry. We stay aboard for five hours and are sent to an army transport that is picking up POW's from all over northern Japan.

14

Coming Home

We arrive in Yokohama Harbor on September 2nd, 1945, and all the ship's men line the rails and salute us as we go past. It was a great feeling, as I thought they had forgotten all about us. Things move fast and a LST {landing craft} pulls up alongside. I am one of the first to go aboard. I bid my shipmates goodbye and say, "I'll see you in the states." I am lucky as this is the only group to be flown to Guam {Navy} and the Philippines {Army}, about a twelve-hour trip. The hardest thing to get used to is the freedom, if you can call Navy life freedom.

Arriving at Guam, it looks like a major U.S. city. The last time I was there in 1939, there was no airfield and no dock. In 1939, we had to take a small steam launch ashore. Wow! What a change, and how much I had missed. I felt out of place and did so for a long time after. Strange feelings were overtaking me that I didn't understand.

At Guam, we are given tans, socks, shoes, and an oversea hat and underwear. We are examined and found fit for duty. Ha! I weigh a little over one hundred pounds. I stay on Guam for 12 days until September 22nd, 1945.

Every day a list is put up for air transport back to the USA. I get tired of waiting, so bold as brass, I put my name down on the bottom of the list. It works. I fly. My buddies come back by ship fifteen days later. It was one twelve-hour hop to Kawjelean, where we have lunch, and another twelve hour flight to Honolulu, where we are put up at a Naval hospital. The next day the nurse says I have a visitor and tells me to stay put because he is on his way up.

I look down the ward toward the entrance and, lo and behold my older brother, Harry, appears. I don't recognize him at first, as he has put on a lot of weight. We talk for a while and then he asks me if I have any money. I had just drawn $300 that morning, so I give him $150, as I have no use for it and he does. In typical Navy fashion, they hadn't paid him in months. When you got transferred and they failed to transfer your pay records, sometimes it took months to get paid. They wouldn't pay you without a record and it took a while for the record to get transferred. He said he had been stationed on a ship as an armed guard traveling through the war zone. He had made a lot of runs up to Russia in the early part of the war, when German subs were sinking half the ships going up there. When the war ended, he had enough points for discharge. They dropped him off in Honolulu at the airport. He hadn't been paid in quite a long time.

As I mentioned before, we came from a large family. There were thirteen children; nine boys and four girls. I was somewhere in the middle. After the first contact with the family, Harry found out that our brothers, Roy, Walter, and Art were also in the Navy. He didn't know where they were stationed. Apparently, I started a family trend.

I rest in Honolulu for two days and have a hard time sleeping in a bed. I have to sleep on the floor. All the time in the Navy {7 ½ years}, except in the hospital on two occasions, I had never slept in a bed. When we were in the POW camps, we used to sleep on flat straw mats on top of boards. With the POW days behind me, I wonder what awaits me back home.

I spend a few days in the Naval Hospital in Honolulu and then I fly to Oakland, California. I am placed in Oak Knoll Hospital.

On the first night back, a Chief by the name of Harry Clark asks me, "As long as I wasn't going ashore, would I hold his money belt?"

It has $8000 in it, which was a lot of money at that time. I said yes and put it around my waist. Then, at about 11pm, a couple of shipmates approach me.

They say, "Come on, Andy, let's go ashore! We haven't done anything for years!"

So, I go ashore.

The first thing I know, I am feeling rosy in Sweet's Ballroom. I fell asleep on one of the sofas that lined the walls. At about 2am I am put in a cab and sent back to the hospital. The next morning, Harry asks me for the money.

He said, "You son-of-a-bitch! You went ashore! Where's my money belt?"

I said, "Geez, I don't know." I had forgotten all about it. Luckily, it was still there.

Harry was about fifty years old from Dorchester, MA. He had not been back to the states in thirty years. Before the war, he owned two bars in Shanghai and had four Chinese wives and a bunch of kids. When the war broke out in September, 1942, the Navy called him back into service, as he was in the fleet reserve. At that time, he weighed over four hundred pounds. He said he drank a quart of whiskey a day and had cirrhosis of the liver. When he weighed in at Guam upon liberation, he weighed one hundred and five pounds, while I weighed one hundred pounds. During his time in prison, he lived off his fat. I remember one time he took his clothes off and he had a flap of flesh that hung down from his chest down over his knees. Over time, this tightened up and his time as a POW made him healthy. He felt like a new man. His liver was now working fine. He said he was going back to China as soon as he could, but first he was going to see the family he left behind in the states—same story.

The day after I went ashore in Oakland, CA, my youngest brother, Walter, comes and we have a visit. We go ashore and the bar serves him, but they think I am too young. All I have for an ID is a card saying I am a returned POW. Everything is okay after I show them that. Walter had doctored his ID, making him 21 years old instead of his actual age, 20. He brought me up to date about the family. Where would I stay when I arrived home?

Apparently, the three youngest children in the family had lost their home to Henry and Harry, the oldest. Henry had a wife and nine children and had taken over the house with his twin, Harry. Harry was a bachelor, but he used to boss everyone around. I guess they turned my sister, Evelyn, and her husband, "Red" Jackson, out. I never did find out why. I ended up living with my brother, Roy, in Everett, MA for about a year. My younger brother, Walter, stayed there too.

I leave Oakland, CA about November, 1945. I fly in a C-47 to Winslow, Arizona. Wow! There are planes stacked up here as far as the eye can see. I guess the USA over-built. Then, on to Newton, Kansas. I stay there overnight and am tempted to go to Wichita, the place where I made my best liberty in the Navy. I decide against it, as I am anxious to get home.

The next day, I fly to Floyd Bennett Field, NYC. I check my parachute in and take a bus to Grand Central Station.

While waiting to board a train to Boston, a little old lady {forty-something} says, "Son, you don't have to stand in line."

So, I go by a special gate for servicemen and take her along, bypassing the very long line. My how things had changed compared to peacetime. On the train to Boston, a woman hands me her infant to hold, while she goes off. I thought that was the greatest compliment and trust I ever had. On October 3rd, 1945 I finally meet my family in Everett, Massachusetts. Home at last.

15

The Aftermath

When I arrived home, I found out about the status of my brothers in the Navy. My brother, Arthur, had joined the Navy in the middle of 1941, before the war broke out. My brother, Roy, joined the Navy in 1942. My oldest brother, Harry, and my youngest brother, Walter, enlisted in the Navy in 1943. Walter joined up as soon as he turned eighteen. My brother, Harry, was thirty-eight years old when he entered the Navy. Walter was just starting boot camp as Harry was leaving. When he finished boot camp at age thirty-eight, you would think they would give him a relatively easy assignment. Instead, they assigned him to a merchant ship as an armed guard. That was a hell of a place to put a guy at his age. At the time, the merchant ships were getting sunk at an unprecedented rate.

Ironically, my youngest brother, Walter, crossed paths with my younger brother, Arthur, while they were carrying out their various Navy duties during World War II. Arthur was waiting on a dock in Recife, Brazil when Walter arrived to serve with the same unit Arthur was leaving.

We were supposed to "report in" to get a new assignment after we arrived in Boston. One former American POW didn't report in until two years later. Technically, he was right because the Navy never gave us a date we had to report in by. He spent two years attending classes at Boston University and then reported in. He said, "I didn't know we were supposed to report in". They paid him two years of back pay.

When I returned to Boston, they gave me six months of leave. I thought I was getting a great deal until I figured out that I hadn't had any leave in over six years. The only thing I had to do during my leave was to check in with a medical doctor for an hour every week. My younger brother, Walter, got out of the Navy in March, 1946, and used to ride with me to the doctor every week. I told my brother that the doctors must have thought I was crazy because of the head injury I received at the smelter plant in Wakasaning. Eventually, a new doctor replaced

104

my old doctor and he must have figured out I wasn't crazy, because he told me I didn't have to come any more.

When I finally made it back home, it took me a long time just to walk down the street and feel comfortable. I didn't feel comfortable doing anything. I don't know what it was, but it took me a long time getting used to living again. I was used to being under somebody's thumb for twenty-four hours a day. I didn't realize what was happening at the time. Back then, there was no counseling to help me figure out what was going on.

It was two or three years before I felt safe and secure. I didn't feel right just walking down the street. It was a terrible feeling. I didn't know what was going on in my mind. I didn't know why I felt that way. In retrospect, I think maybe I subconsciously felt like I was doing something wrong by roaming around freely. When I was in the POW camp, I would never be able to walk around freely. I had somebody looking over my shoulder all the time. In order to survive in the POW camp, I had to train my mind to give up all my freedoms and go into a strict, undeviating routine. If I had decided to walk freely around in the shipyard or the POW camp, I would have been killed. So, when I was in the states walking around freely, my mind was still trained to think I was doing something dangerous that could get me killed. I thought I would get over this feeling much faster than I did.

When I first got back to the states, I had trouble sleeping. I could stay up 24 hours a day without a problem. I used to stay up all night drinking, stay awake all day, and then stay up all night drinking again. I could do this for days at a time. I think one of the reasons I was unable to sleep was because I didn't want to miss anything. I wanted to savor every moment of freedom. They had to give me tranquilizers to get to sleep. When I was married seven years later, I still didn't sleep well. My wife, Penny, found it hard to sleep in the same bed with me because I was so restless.

I had a good connection that was steering me in the direction of re-enlistment. Pop Lundberg's brother was a campaign manager for a Senator in New Hampshire. The Senator had a lot of influence and was the Chairman of the Armed Services Committee in 1945. Pop told me to come down to Washington with him and he would get me a commission as a Chief Warrant Officer.

Those were tough times for my mind back then because I really wasn't thinking clearly. I finally decided to follow my instincts and do what I wanted to do. I was tired of having other people tell me what to do all the time. In the military, everywhere you turn, someone is telling you what to do. It was always a relief to get away from the military routine. Everyone likes to be their own boss and control their own life. That's the way it should be.

Nine months after returning to the U.S., I decided to take a discharge from the Navy. I got out on June 15th, 1946. I wanted to start living my life again. My buddies and I had been through a lot. We endured experiences most people can't imagine. Back in the POW camps, it was sometimes tempting to give up and quit. My friends and I never gave up. We never surrendered.

Some POWs stayed in Japan after they were liberated and went looking for their former prison guards to get some payback. My attitude was "I want to forget about this. I don't want to talk about it. I don't want to remember it." When I returned to the states, I met with Naval Intelligence for a period of fifteen days and they asked me about my experiences as a POW. I refused to talk about it. I wanted to forget it. It was over and done with and I wanted to move on.

My family told me they received a telegram in late 1943, notifying them that I was still alive. Apparently, a woman in Oregon picked up a short-wave radio message broadcast by the Japanese, which included my name on a list of POW's. The woman notified the Navy and the Navy sent a telegram to my family.

When I went back and saw my family, they said, "Gee, we were awfully worried about you."

I said, "There was nothing to worry about. I knew I was alive."

Epilogue

Before leaving the Navy, my great uncle and war hero, Earl Anderson, was awarded the Purple Heart for the abuse he suffered in the Japanese prison camps. In 1994 Earl was awarded the bronze star for his heroic fighting in the Philippines.

You might wonder what happened to my great uncle after he left the Navy. Although he had difficulty and great pain adjusting to life out of a prison camp—feeling out of place during the day and unable to sleep well at night—he never surrendered. Two weeks after being discharged from the Navy, he and his friend, Gene Gagnon, bought a nightclub in Grafton. After hiring a good band, crowds of customers, mostly from the nearby mills, came to the club. Even a local mafia leader frequently came with his girlfriend. When he learned Earl had a large basement in his club, he wanted to start a card-playing gambling operation there. Although Earl's partner wanted to make money from the project, Earl vetoed the deal. He felt that once you were in with the mafia, you were in forever. For two years the business went well until the mills in the area went south and the nightclub folded.

Seeking a more stable life, Earl began working at the Charlestown Navy Yard where he stayed until he retired in 1964. While at the Navy Yard, he met a fun loving woman, Penny Scovli, to whom he was married for 52 years. Although Penny helped my great uncle to overcome many of the demons that haunted him from his inhumane and atrocious treatment in the concentration camps, he always slept restlessly. Even today Earl doesn't sleep peacefully.

After retiring in 1964, Earl and Penny traveled extensively throughout the United States. Earl sold his house and bought a traveling trailer. For the next six years, they traveled all over the United States, Canada, and Mexico. They spent two fun filled winters in Mexico, enjoying the friendliness of the people. Mardi Gras was a fun event with singing, dancing, drinking, and fireworks in the streets. One firework hit a curb and bounced through a hotel window, starting a conflagration. In spite of the raging fire and responding fire engines, the party continued unabated.

The couple toured Europe several times beginning in 1971. In 1988 Earl and Penny took a trip to China, revisiting some old haunts. The changes were spectacular. The International Settlement in Shanghai was obviously no longer European. The hotel he stayed at when he was in the Navy was still standing. He found out the Chinese still hated the Japanese for their brutal war crimes against the Chinese people. When he was asked if he also hated the Japanese, Earl responded that he "didn't care" for the Japanese because "they never set the record straight" about their wartime atrocities against the American, British, Filipino, and Chinese people.

In 2005, after 52 years of a happy marriage, Penny died from Alzheimer's Disease. For the last five years of her life, Earl personally cared for her as she slowly lost her memory to this debilitating disease.

Currently, Earl lives a quiet life in his home in Summerfield, Florida. He frequently has breakfast at McDonald's with his brother Walter, who now lives nearby and was also in the Navy during World War II, and some other good friends. Ironically, one of the members of the unofficial McDonald's meeting group is George Smith, former POW Hank Henderson's brother-in-law.

Every Wednesday he has a few drinks socializing with his friends at a club for singles in his housing association. He enjoys watching the news and weather on TV. He thinks Bill O'Reilly is a pretty straight shooter.

Earl is now 87 years old and still surviving and happy to be living in the "Good Ole U.S.A." He has never surrendered. He is a true Hero to me.

Shawn Davis

Author Bios

Earl Anderson was born in 1919 to Swedish immigrant parents in Everett, Massachusetts. He was the third youngest of 13 children, {9 boys and 4 girls}. Five of the brothers served in the U.S. Navy in World War II. Earl joined the Navy on January 26th, 1938, with high hopes of making it a career.

After graduating from Boot Camp and Machinist School, Earl was stationed in the Asiatic Fleet in China and the Philippines. He served on both the U.S.S. Canopus {submarine tender}, and the U.S.S. Permit {submarine}. He was stationed at Olongapo when the Japanese attacked Pearl Harbor on December 7th, 1941. Earl miraculously survived bombardments by land, air and sea, until he and his buddies were forced to abandon and sink ship in Mariveles Bay on April 7th, 1942, a day before the surrender of U.S. forces on Bataan. Earl and squad were then assigned to augment the Marines' beach defenses on the heavily fortified island of Corregidor. They fought against superior Japanese forces until the U.S. surrendered on May 7th, 1942. At that time, Earl became a P.O.W. of the Japanese for three and a half years.

Earl returned to the states in late September, 1945. He suffered from what we now know as Post Traumatic Stress Disorder, but adapted as best as he could. The following year Earl made the decision to leave the Navy and worked in the Charlestown Navy Yard until his retirement in 1964 when he began traveling the world. Earl rarely spoke of his experiences in the Navy and as a POW. In the year 2000, his nephew, Earl Wayne Jackson, convinced Earl to write about his real life adventures. Earl wrote a forty-page synopsis of his WW II experiences. In April, 2005, another one of Earl's nephews, Bill Davis, attended a family reunion event and became fascinated by Earl's story. Bill Davis enlisted his son, Shawn, an aspiring writer, to help Earl turn his memoir into a book. After many hours of interviews, Shawn and Earl completed the true-life story, *Never Surrender*, in July, 2006.

Shawn Davis is Earl Anderson's great nephew. He began working on bringing Earl's story to light in April, 2005. Shawn transformed Earl's forty-page narrative and more than twenty hours of interviews into the non-fiction novel, *Never Surrender*. Shawn is also the co-author of the futuristic sociopolitical thriller, *Ameri-*

can Insurrection {currently unpublished}, which is about a large-scale, violent future rebellion in the United States. Shawn majored in English at a New England college and is currently working on a degree in Criminal Justice. Shawn is a Campus Police Lieutenant at a college in Massachusetts. He is currently working on the edgy crime thriller, *American Criminal.*

Bibliography for Never Surrender

Battle for Iwo Jima, www.geocities.com/Pentagon/7338/usmc.html

The Battle of Iwo Jima, www.iwojima.com, 2005

Basic Facts on the Nanjing Massacre and the Tokyo War Crimes Trial, cnd.org/mjmassacre/nj.html

Bradley, James, Powers, Ron, Flags of Our Fathers:Heroes of Iwo Jima, Bantam Doubleday Dell Books for Young Readers, 2003

Chang, Iris, The Rape of Nanking: The Forgotten Holocaust of World War II, BasicBooks, 1997

Commemorating the 60th Anniversary of the Nanking Massacre {1937-1938}, www.princeton.edu/nanking/html/main.html

Craven, W.L., J.L.Cate, The Army Air Forces in World War II: Plans and Early Operations January 1939 to August 1942, www.ibiblio.org/hyperwar/AAF/I/AAF-I-6.html

Eyewitness to History, Attack at Pearl Harbor, 1941, www.eyewitnesstohistory.com/pearl.htm

GlobalSecurity.org, Battle of Okinawa, www.globalsecurity.org/military/facility/okinawa-battle.htm

Glusman, John A., Conduct Under Fire: Four American Doctors and Their Fight for Life as Prisoners of the Japanese, Viking Penguin, NY, 2005

Guadalcanal, www.army.mil/cmh-pg/brochures/72-82.htm

A Guadalcanal Chronology, www.friesian.com/history/guadal.htm

Henderson, Henry Clay, U.S.N., The Diary of Henry Clay Henderson, 1998, www.mississipi.net/~comcents/tendertale.com

The History Teacher, The Battle of Okinawa, 1945: Final Turning Point in the Pacific, 2000, www.historycooperative.org/journals/ht/34.l/tzeng.html,

Internet Modern History Sourcebook, The Nanking Massacre, 1937, www.fordham.edu/halsall/mod/nanking.html

Miller, J. Michael, From Shanghai to Corregidor: Marines in the Defense of the Philippines, www.nps.gove/wapa/indepth/extContent/usmc/pcn-190-003140-001sec1.htm

Mills, Ami Chen, Breaking the Silence, www.metroactive.com/papers/metro/12.12.96/cover/china1-9650.html

Nanking Massacre: The Forgotten Holocaust, www.gotvain.com/dan/nanking1.htm

National Iwo Jima Monument, www.webtravels.com/iwojima/

National Public Radio, The Battle for Guadalcanal, www.npr.org/programs/re/archivesdate/2002/aug/guadalcanal

Okinawa: the Last Battle, www.army.mil/cmh-pg/books/wwii/okinawa, 2001

Online Naval Historical Center, www.history.;navy.mil

The Rape of Nanking: An Undeniable History in Photographs, www.tribo.org/nanking/

The Rape of Nanking, www.bergen.org/AAST/Projects/ChinaHistory/rape.html

Sackett, E.L., U.S.N., The Canopus, www.shill-family.org/canopustext.html
Stinnett, Robert B., Day of Deceit: the Truth About FDR and Pearl Harbor, Simon and Schuster, New York, 2005

Wikipedia, Attack on Pearl Harbor,
en.wikipedia.org/wiki/Attack_on_Pearl_Harbor,
2005

Wikipedia, Battle of Guadalcanal, en.wikipedia.org/wiki/Battle_of_Guadalcanal

Wikipedia, Battle of Okinawa, www.en.wikipedia.org/wiki/Battle_of_Okinawa

Wikipedia, Nanking Massacre, en.wikipedia.org/wiki/Nanjing-Massacre

978-0-595-40739-
0-595-40739-0

3997821

Made in the USA
Lexington, KY
14 December 2009